White-embroidered costume accessories

The 1790s to 1840s

by Heather Toomer

with drawings and patterns by Elspeth Reed

Contents

Acknowledgments

We are extremely grateful to all the museum staff involved in this task for their willing and patient help and encouragement over several years. In particular we must mention: Anita Blythe (Worcestershire Collection, Hartlebury Castle); Alison Carter, Sarah Howard and Sue Washington (formerly of Hampshire Museums Services); Julia Fox (Devonshire Collection of Period Costume, Totnes); Estelle Gilbert (The Museum of Somerset, Taunton); Isobel Gilpin (Museum of Fashion, Blandford Forum); Miles Lambert (Gallery of Fashion, Platt Hall, Manchester); Kate Loubser (Worthing Museum and Art Gallery); Catherine Littlejohn (Blaise Castle House Museum, Bristol); Althea MacKenzie (Hereford Museum & Art Gallery); Rebecca Quinton (Glasgow Museums, the Burrell Collection); Pauline Rushton (Walker Museum and Art Gallery); Caroline Alexander (Harris Museum and Art Gallery, Preston); Shelley Tobin (Exeter Museums); Elaine Utley (Museum of Fashion, Bath); Linda Wicks (Carrow House Costume and Textile Study Centre, Norwich); members of the Fulneck Moravian Settlement, Leeds.

We also express our thanks to the following institutions for their kind permission to study, photograph and/or reproduce articles in their collections:
Blaise Castle House Museum, Bristol - *Plates II.175, II.212*
Museum of Fashion, Blandford Forum - *Plates II.141, II.195*
Devonshire Collection of Period Costume, Totnes - *Plates II.24, II.164, II.165*
Exeter University Library - *Plates II.11, II.41, II.43*
Fulneck Moravian Settlement, Pudsey, Leeds - *Plates II.203, 203a*
Glasgow Museums, the Burrell collection - *Plate II.183*
Hampshire County Council Museums & Archives Service - *Plates II.37, II.156, II.227*
Harris Museum and Art Gallery, Preston - *Plates II.18, II.42,* II.44, II.65, II.67, II.70, II.98, II.116, II.143, II.178, II.180, II.242
Hereford Museum & Art Gallery - *Plates I.23, II.1, II.2, II.3, II.5, II.21, II.29, II.35, II.36, II.40, II.47, II.48, II.66, II.92, II.119, II.120, II.125, II.126*
Lawrence House Museum, Launceston, Cornwall - *Plate II.163*
Leeds Museums and Galleries (Abbey House) - *Plate II.86*
Manchester City Galleries, Gallery of Fashion, Platt Hall - *Plates II.49, 49a*
Mercer Art Gallery, Harrogate - *Plates II.102, II.113*
Museum of Somerset, Taunton - *Plates II.45, II.51, II.251*
National Museums and Galleries of Wales (Museum of Welsh Life, St. Fagans, Cardiff) - *Plates II.93, II.108*
Walker Museum & Art Gallery, Liverpool - *Plates I.24, II.150*
Worcestershire collection, Hartlebury Castle, Kidderminster - *Plates II.100, 100a*
Worthing Museum and Art Gallery - *Plates II.20, 20a, II.39, II.55a, 55b, II.216*

We should also particularly like to thank the **Textile Society** and the **Southern Counties Costume Society** for their bursaries towards reproduction fees and travelling expenses for our research.

Very special thanks are also due to Alan and Vanessa Hopkins, Harry Matthews, and the late Ann Mary Johnstone for allowing us to borrow, pattern and photograph articles from their collections and to Penelope Byrde Ruddock for reading and advising on the draft. Last, but not least, thanks are due to our husbands Clive Toomer and Martin Reed for their forbearance and encouragement throughout and particularly to Clive Toomer for proof-reading at various stages in the work.

Abbreviations used in this book

Measurements: *(all maximum unless otherwise stated)*
CB - *centre back;* CF - *centre front;* D - *depth;* L - *length;*
Ls - *length of side;* W - *width;* AS - *actual size.*

Public collections
Blaise Castle - *Blaise Castle House Museum, Bristol*
Devonshire Collection - *Devonshire Collection of Period
    Costume, Totnes*
Hampshire collection - *Hampshire County Council Museums &
    Archives Service, Chilcomb House, Winchester*
Harris M & AG - *Harris Museum and Art Gallery, Preston*
Hereford M & AG - *Hereford Museum & Art Gallery*
Platt Hall, Manchester - *Manchester City Galleries, Gallery of
    Fashion, Platt Hall, Manchester*
St. Fagans - *National Museums and Galleries of Wales, Museum
    of Welsh Life, St. Fagans, Cardiff*
V&A - *Victoria & Albert Museum, London*
Walker M & AG - *Walker Museum & Art Gallery, Liverpool*
Worcester collection - *Worcestershire collection, Hartlebury
    Castle, Kidderminster*
Worthing M & AG - *Worthing Museum and Art Gallery*

Pattern scales
Patterns are drawn on $\frac{1}{8}$ in squares to a scale of $\frac{1}{8}$ in = 1in
except for the cuffs (p100) which are to a scale of $\frac{1}{4}$ in = 1in.

Preface

I bought my first 1830s whiteworked pelerine in Torquay,
Devon. It was one of those happy days when I took my
elderly friend Kathleen first to the Newton Abbot weekly
antiques market, then on to Torquay, Dartmouth, Exeter or
Totnes, all of which had shops or markets where we might
find lace or embroidery.

In those days, about 20-30 years ago, we could always
guarantee to buy a few items. We went round venues in
opposite directions so as not to compete and later, when
back at Kathleen's home for tea, we would get out our
purchases and share our pleasure. Often the room was
covered in white and we could marvel at the sheer variety of
design and texture it afforded and the exquisiteness of the
workmanship.

Lace always took priority then. We could neither of us afford
to buy everything we saw but, gradually, our whitework
collections also grew.

As the market changed and antique shops disappeared in
favour of fairs, there were still numerous dealers in antique
clothes and textiles who included lace and whitework in
their stock. Now the picture is very different. Admittedly I
want better, more specialist pieces than when I started but
fine, white, hand-worked textiles are no longer so readily
available. Perhaps the lull in the market is purely temporary
or perhaps too many items have now been cut, re-used and
discarded.

I hope that readers of this book will endeavour, like me, to
save what remains.

Introduction

As a sequel to our previous work, 'Embroidered with white: the 18th-century fashion for Dresden lace and other whiteworked accessories', this book continues the story of women's decorative white accessories through from the very end of the 18th century to the 1840s. During this period, the slow evolution of women's fashion that had been the norm through much of the 18th century changed to a quicker pace and the more rapid developments in dress were complemented by equally rapid changes in accessories.

At the beginning of our period, about 1790, the stiff fashions of the early-mid 18th century had already given way to softer lines and, by the late 1790s, dress was much slimmer. Flowing whiteworked sleeve ruffles, worn as accessories for much of the 18th century, had effectively disappeared and whiteworked aprons were less in evidence. Neck handkerchiefs, or kerchiefs, still provided a little warmth and modesty around the neckline, or were draped artistically over the head, but long shawls and complex, frilled alternatives, often in bright colours, proved a popular contrast to the white of much fashionable dress. Thus, as demands of fashion changed, some accessories disappeared only to be replaced by others.

By the 1790s a new accessory had already developed that could not be accommodated in our earlier book: this was the habit shirt, or chemisette, as it later became known. Although originally similar to a man's shirt, by the end of the century a sleeveless version had evolved which was open under the arms and usually fastened by strings around the waist. We shall follow this item through its various transformations in the 19th century as it takes over some of the rôle of the kerchief in filling in a low neckline and providing that decorous layer of washable, white fabric next to the skin. The chemisette was one of the many new accessories to gain importance in the 19th century. Its early standing bands developed into falling collars which might be made as separate accessories. As these spread over the widening shoulder line of the 1820s-30s, they transmuted into small capes, or pelerines, while smaller whiteworked collars might still be fashionable as an upper layer. All these varied accessories might be accompanied by matching cuffs.

With the collapse of the shoulder line in the later 1830s, wide-spreading pelerines gave way to fichus, capes and large shawls that wrapped tightly around the body. Handkerchiefs that were truly carried in the hand also gained importance. The types of whiteworked accessory worn in the first half of the 19th century thus changed but it was not only their cut and shaping that changed, it was also their decoration. By the 1790s the complex Dresden work that had been all the rage in the early-to-mid 18th century had become outmoded and had been replaced by simpler designs influenced by neo-classical taste and worked in a smaller variety of stitches. Starting from this simple beginning, new embroidery styles arose in the 19th century and patterns and stitching again grew fuller and more diverse.

As in the 18th century, white headwear was also fashionable in the 19th century but the enormous variety of caps and bonnets worn in the early 1800s cannot be accommodated alongside other accessories in a book of this size. Many such items can, however, be seen in books on hats and headwear while the changes in embroidery styles discussed in the following pages are equally applicable to them.

A further exclusion from this book is menswear. At the beginning of our period men might still wear shirts with ruffled fronts but these were usually of plain fabric. Embroidered white waistcoats and women's stomachers were largely a thing of the past, with quilting and heavier forms of whitework, such as Mountmellick work, reserved mainly for furnishing fabrics: such works do not have a place here.

A final restriction is to accessories made from woven fabrics, mostly muslins or firmer cottons but occasionally linens or pina cloths. By the early 19th century machine nets had been invented and embroidery techniques were quickly applied to them. The new products can be classified as whitework and were used for similar accessories but they were also designed and used as alternatives to lace. Theirs is yet another story that will be left for a future work.

Section I

A BRIEF RÉSUMÉ OF CHANGING STYLES OF WOMEN'S DRESS AND WHITEWORKED ACCESSORIES FROM 1795 TO 1845

The basic changes in women's fashions through the 19th century have been described and illustrated in numerous books on the subject and it would be otiose to describe them here in detail. The following sketches are provided, however, for readers unfamiliar with their story and to show the particular contribution made to the changing fashionable look by whiteworked accessories.

A word of warning

These sketches accord with a timescale drawn from the numerous fashion illustrations of the period: the reality was far more complex. The actual dates at which change occurred varied with the wearers' tastes, age and position in society: the aristocracy and wealthy bourgeoisie were generally the first to take up new ideas and these spread gradually into the remaining population over a number of years.

Rules of etiquette also demanded that different styles of dress and accessory be worn at different times of day and year but compliance with such rules depended on the personal lifestyle of the wearer. Thus an enormous variety of accessories and embroidery styles might be seen in any one year and one cannot be too precise in ascribing dates to surviving accessories. Even when they accord closely with surviving dated patterns, those patterns may have been used over several years.

1. c1795: a long-sleeved day dress with narrow frills at the wrists and a kerchief tucked into the low neckline.

2. c1800: a high-waisted, trained neo-classical day gown with long sleeves. The low neckline is filled in with a habit shirt, or chemisette, with a standing collar supporting a small ruff.

3. c1810: a neo-classical day gown with an even more slender silhouette and ankle-length skirt. A long shawl gives a sense of flowing drapery.

4. c1815: a low-necked day gown worn over a chemisette with a triple vandyked ruff. The waistline is still high but the sleeves are slightly puffed at the shoulders and the skirt is A-line.

5. c1825: a day gown with a slightly lower waistline, bell-shaped skirt and fuller sleeves. A white muslin collar, possibly attached to a chemisette, extends from high around the neck onto the shoulders.

6. c1830: a day gown with a fuller bell-shaped skirt. A double pelerine with vandyked edges spreads from high around the neck onto the full sleeve heads; whiteworked cuffs decorate the wrists.

7. c1835: a day gown with an almost natural waistline, even fuller bell-shaped skirt and gigot sleeves. A double pelerine spreads from high around the neck right over the full sleeve heads and has lappets hanging down the front and caught under the belt at the waist.

8. c1840: a day gown with sleeves tight over the shoulders and with fullness above the elbows worn over a chemisette with a shawl collar that covers the edges of the V-shaped neckline.

9. c1845: a full-skirted day gown worn with a collared fichu which accentuates the shaping of the bodice into a dropped waistline at the front. White undersleeves fill the gap between the ends of the shortened sleeves and the wrists.

c1795   c1800   c1810   c1815   c1825

c1830   c1835   c1840   c1845

GLOSSARY PART I:
Embroidery stitches and terms

Appliqué work
Work in which a cord, fabric or other artefact is sewn on to the surface of a fabric: overcasting stitches are usually used to hold the cut edges of applied fabrics or cords

*Plate I.1 (above) Right side of **appliqué work**: denser pattern areas comprise **two layers of fabric** which contrast with the single layer of the ground. The two layers are sewn together with running stitches covered by overcasting around outlines and lines within the design: one layer around the motifs is cut away after the two layers have been sewn together.*

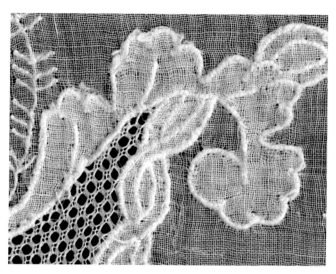

*Plate I.1a (above) Wrong side of the **appliqué work** in Plate I.1*

*Plate I.2 (left) Right side of **appliqué work** with an applied pre-made braid attached by simple running stitches invisible on the right side.*

*Plate I.2a (bottom right) Wrong side of the **appliqué work** in Plate I.2 showing running stitches holding the braid which is visible through the semi-transparent fabric.*

Ayrshire work

The work usually associated with the name arose in the 1810s and consists of fine whitework embroidery in floral designs worked mainly in padded satin stitch. Fillings are of needlepoint lace stitches in the best work and pulled-thread work in cheaper forms. In the late 18th-early 19th centuries Ayrshire produced tambour work.

Plate I.3 (below) An Ayrshire embroidery with typical fine stitching in padded satin stitch with spaces filled with needlepoint lace stitches. Fillings could alternatively be of pulled-thread work. See also Plate I.11.

Back stitch

A stitch forming a continuous line of short stitches on one side, normally the right side, of a fabric and a row of longer, overlapping stitches on the reverse.

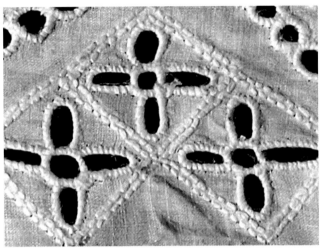

Plate I.4 (above) Two lines of back stitches form diamond shapes surrounding overcast eyelets.

Plate I.4a (below) The wrong side of the work in Plate I.4.

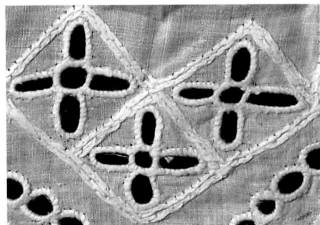

Blanket stitch and related stitches

Blanket stitch (basic – usually used in plain sewing rather than embroidery) An L-shaped stitch with a base and upright of equal length at right angles to each other: the bases form a continuous line. In variations, the bases and uprights may be of different lengths and at an angle other than 90° to each other.

Buttonhole stitch (closely worked blanket stitch) I am following the practice of many embroidery and lace books in using this term for blanket stitch worked with the uprights so close together that they touch although this is not the true, or tailor's, buttonhole stitch which has an extra twist in it. Buttonhole stitch is commonly used to finish cut fabric edges as it forms a strong outline. It is also the basic stitch for needlepoint fillings. (See Plate I.11)

*Plate I.6 (above) The right sides of two layers of vandyked fabric: the right-hand edge is neatened with simple **buttonhole stitches** while the edge in the centre is neatened with graduated **buttonhole stitches** approaching the smoothness of the buttonholed satin stitches in Plate I.7. The leaf design is in padded satin stitch with a trailed stem.*

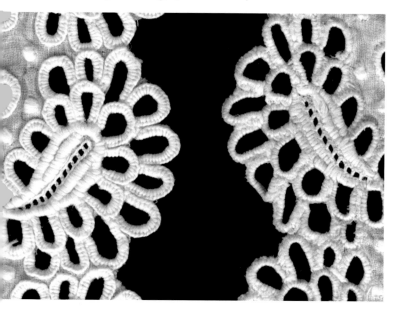

*Plate I.5 (above) **Buttonhole stitches** strengthening a cut outer edge and cut edges of holes in an embroidery: the right side is on the left and the wrong side on the right. The ridged outline created by buttonhole stitches on the right side is clear. The centre of the motif is filled with **ladder stitch**.*

Buttonholed satin stitch Buttonhole stitches worked with long stems, often of graduated lengths, so as to cover an area like satin stitch but with one distinct, firm edge; usually used in the 19th century to strengthen edges rather than as a decorative surface stitch as in the 18th century. It is often worked over slight padding: when used to form a scalloped edge it may simply be called **'scalloping'**.

Buttonholed eyelet An eyelet, or hole, surrounded by buttonhole stitches used either to stop a cut edge from fraying or to keep a pierced but uncut hole open. (See Plate I.8)

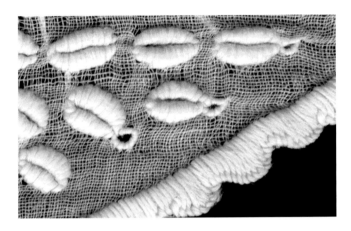

*Plate I.7 (above) 'Scalloping': an edge neatened with carefully graduated **buttonholed satin stitches** forming slight scallops. The oval spots are in **veined padded satin stitch**. See Plate I.8 for scalloping being worked.*

*Plate I.7a (below) The wrong side of the **scalloped** edge in Plate I.7: the ridged edge on the right side does not show on the reverse.*

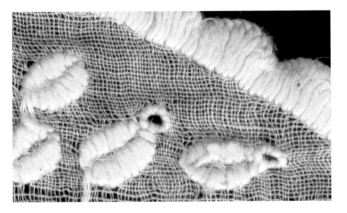

Broderie anglaise A cutwork embroidery consisting of a multitude of holes of simple, repetitive shapes arranged to form a decorative pattern. The edges of the holes are usually strengthened by overcasting but may be buttonholed, particularly along the fabric borders.

*Plate I.8 (above) Detail from an unfinished **broderie anglaise**. Long **running stitches**, just visible on some blue lines of the pattern, outline the holes before they are overcast or buttonholed. The oval holes have overcast edges: the round holes have buttonholed edges. The outer edge is 'scalloped'.*
Here the holes are cut after the embroidery is worked but they can be stamped out beforehand: the edge is normally cut afterwards.

Buttonhole stitches –
see under **'Blanket stitch'**

Chain stitch A line of looped stitches looking like a chain: it may be worked with **a needle or with a tambour hook** or, from the 1830s, by machine: the results are almost identical on the right side of the work. **Split stitch** can also look similar on the right side. For an excellent exposition of the differences between needle-worked and tamboured chain stitch, see Gail Marsh's '18th Century Embroidery Techniques', Guild of Master Craftsmen Publications Ltd., 2006

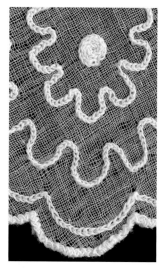

Cording – see *'Trailing'*

Couching – see *'Overcasting'*

Counted-thread work Embroidery in which stitches are placed extremely accurately by the counting of threads between positions in which a needle is inserted in a woven fabric: used to create areas of decorative geometric patterning. See **pulled-** and **drawn-thread work** under **'Openwork embroidery'**.

Cutwork Any embroidery, such as broderie anglaise, involving the cutting of holes in a fabric.

Drawn-thread work – see **'Openwork Embroidery'**

Dresden lace/work – see **'Openwork Embroidery'**

Eyelet A small round hole sometimes made for the passage of a cord but also purely for decoration. It may be kept open by various stitches. (See Plates I.4 and I.8)

Filling/Filling stitch A fancy stitch used for decorative effect to fill a space in lace or embroidery. There are numerous counted-thread and needlepoint lace fillings but embroidered net insertions were also used in 19th century work. (See Plates I.15-16 for pulled fillings)

Needlepoint filling A filling made with needlepoint lace stitches (variations on buttonhole stitch) worked across a hole in a design and interlinked so as to fill the hole.

Plate I.9 (top left) *Chain stitches worked with a needle.*

Plate I.9a (top right)
The wrong side of the chain stitches in Plate I.9: the thread does not pass through the fabric in exactly the same place at the beginning and end of each stitch as it does when worked with a tambour hook.

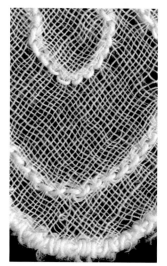

Plate I.10 (left) *Tamboured chain stitch; the right side. Tamboured chain stitch forms the pattern and is also worked over the scalloped edge to neaten it.*

Plate I.10a (bottom) *Tamboured chain stitch; the wrong side. The thread forms a continuous line of straight stitches: it runs in and out of the same hole at each stitch.*

Openwork embroidery

A term for various decorative techniques in which holes are formed in a fabric: **broderie anglaise** has already been seen.

Drawn-thread work A form of open counted-thread embroidery in which some threads are cut and drawn out of a fabric to leave open areas crossed by other threads which are drawn together, strengthened and decorated by embroidery threads: also known as 'pulled-thread work' but, in this book, I am using the term in the manner currently used by the Royal School of Needlework.

Ladder stitch A form of **drawn-thread work** in which a few threads are drawn out and groups of threads crossing the space left are drawn together to form holes separated by bars, like a ladder. (See Plate I.5)

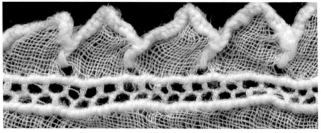

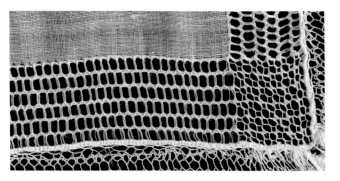

*Plate I.11 (top) A variety of **needlepoint fillings** in an Ayrshire embroidery: the cut edges of the holes containing the fillings are prevented from fraying by padded satin stitches.*

Plate I.12 (middle) An openwork band between trailed lines. Variously-worked narrow openwork bands are often found inside edges. This example has two rows of holes: others have different numbers of rows: the holes can be kept open by different embroidery stitches. Bands may, but need not be, sandwiched between trailed and/ or buttonholed lines. It is often impossible to tell whether they are worked by the 'drawn-thread' or the pulled-thread' technique (p14-15).

Plate I.13 (bottom) A drawn-thread border in which, on the right, some vertical threads are removed and the horizontal threads are drawn together by embroidery threads: the reverse is true along the bottom. In the corner, only a few horizontal threads are left: meshes are formed almost entirely by embroidery threads. The cutting and removal of threads weakens the fabric

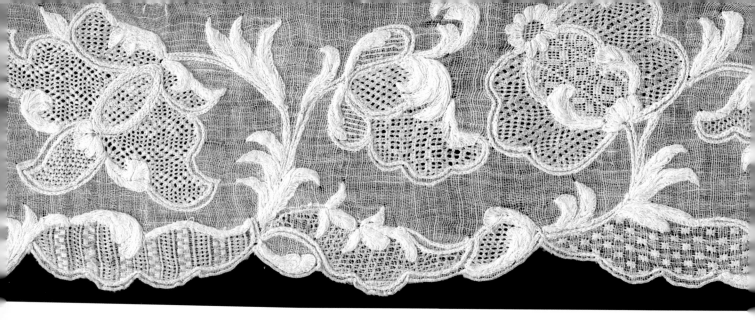

*Plate I.14 (above) Detail from a mid-18th century **Dresden work** including a variety of **pulled-thread** fillings. Designs changed through the century (see our book 'Embroidered with white') but never included the **padded satin stitch** of much 19th-century work.*

Dresden lace/work Name coined in the 19th century for an extremely fine form of 18th century whitework worked in scrolling designs with large, stylised, exotic flowers and leaves, cartouches and strapwork, all incorporating substantial areas of pulled-thread work: the finest examples were made in Dresden and Saxony. Derivatives were also worked in the 19th century.

Pulled-thread work A form of open counted-thread work in which embroidery threads are used to pull the fabric threads apart and create decorative patterns of holes and stitching: also known as 'drawn-thread work' (see above). It is often difficult to distinguish the two techniques in a finished work.

*Plate I.15 (left) Detail from a collar (Plate II.199) showing a 19th- century derivative of Dresden work including floral motifs in padded satin stitch, whipped running and trailing with large areas of **pulled-thread fillings**: the use of padded satin stitch in many 19th-century works distinguishes them from the flatter 18th-century works.*

*Plate I.15a (opposite bottom) Detail from the embroidery in Plate I.15 showing large areas of **pulled-thread work**: the outlined **padded satin stitch** motifs contain tiny **ladder-stitch** fillings.*

Outlined padded satin stitch - see **'Satin stitches'**.
Overcast eyelet An eyelet in which the hole is kept open by overcasting: the hole may be cut or pierced by a stiletto depending on its size. (See Plates I.4 and I.8)
Overcasting A sewing technique in which a series of stitches is worked along a line but with each stitch at an angle to the line: used to prevent a cut edge from fraying; or to hold a thread or cord on a surface in which case it may be called **'couching'**. (See Plates I.1, I.8, I.22)
Padded satin stitch - see **'Satin stitches'**.
Picot A small projecting loop or point often formed to decorate an edge. Picots may be needle-made or may be made in strips with lace bobbins or by machine.
Running stitch A line of stitches worked in and out of a fabric creating alternating stitches and spaces on both right and wrong sides: in decorative work and when forming padding, stitches on the right side are often longer than on the reverse. (See Plate I.8)

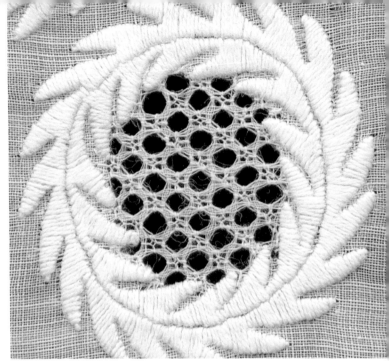

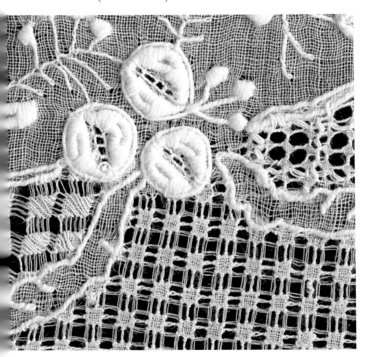

Plate I.16 Satin stitch (above) surrounding a pulled-thread filling. The wrong side is only slightly less neat.

Satin stitches

Basic satin stitch Straight stitches worked closely side by side across a design motif or area so as to cover it completely and form a smooth, satin-like surface.
Buttonholed satin stitch - see under **'Blanket stitch'**
Padded satin stitch Satin stitch worked over padding usually formed by stitches - either satin stitches or running stitches worked transverse the direction of the subsequent satin stitches - which fill the area to be covered. The result is a smooth, raised surface on the right side and a flatter surface on the reverse. (See Plate II.17 and I.17a)
Outlined Padded satin stitch (my term) An area of padded satin stitch surrounded by a narrow overcast line.
(See Plates I.15a, I.18)
Veined padded satin stitch (my term) An area of padded satin stitch divided by a cleft which is used to define a vein in a leaf, an indented edge or some other design feature. (See Plate I.18)

Plate I.17 (above) *The right side of an embroidery with leaves and petals in* ***padded satin stitch****.*

Plate I.18 (below) *Embroidery including pointed leaves in* ***padded satin stitch with central veins and trailed outlines****, round* ***padded satin stitch spots with trailed outlines****,* ***leaves/petals with indented edges and veins****, and an openwork band between trailed lines.*

Plate I.17a (above) *The wrong side of the embroidery in Plate I.17.*

Scalloping Graduated buttonholed satin stitch used to form a scalloped edge - see under **'Blanket stitch – buttonholed satin stitch'**: Plates I.7, I.7a, I.8.
Seed stitch/Seeding Embroidered dots used as a decorative filling. The dots may be made by various stitches, e.g: running stitches with short stitches on the right side; back stitches; chain stitch worked on the wrong side of the fabric; or knotted stitches.

Plate I.19 (below) *Embroidery with* ***seeding*** *created by several back stitches worked alongside each other.*

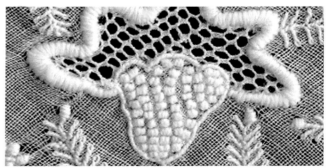

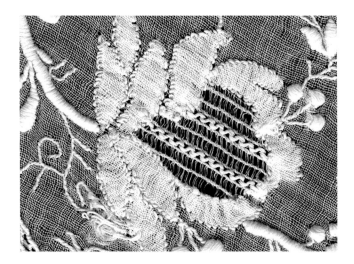

Plate I.20 (above) Shadow work: the right side

Plate I.20a (right top) Shadow work; the wrong side.

Shadow work Embroidery on the wrong side of a semi-transparent fabric that is seen as an opaque area on the right side: usually created by herringbone stitch on the wrong side - seen as a continuous line of minute stitches, like back stitches, around the opaque area on the right.

Split stitch A back stitch in which the needle is brought up through each stitch on the right side to split its thread: the result can look like chain stitch.

Stem stitch A line of stitches worked at a slight angle to the line with each stitch starting halfway along the previous stitch: the two sides look very similar.

Tambour work/Tambouring - see *'Chain stitch'*

Plate I.21 (below) Stem stitch: the right side

Plate I.19a (below) The wrong side of the seeding in Plate I.19.

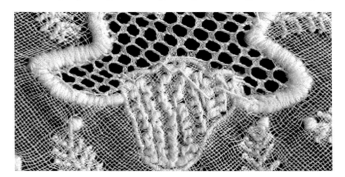

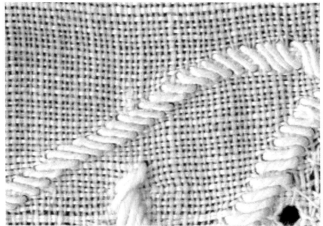

Trailing A solid, slightly raised line of stitching created by overcasting a line of running stitches and/or a laid thread or threads. The working of running stitches in one direction and couching in the reverse enables branching lines or stems to be worked in a continuous process. When worked over laid threads it may be called **'cording'** but as underlying threads are normally completely hidden it is not usually possible to see the substructure in a finished work. The use of more or thicker laid threads gives more pronounced trailed lines.

Whipped running Running stitches in which, once a line has been run, the thread is worked, or whipped, back through the stitches on the surface with a loose overcasting stitch: the overcasting thread should not penetrate the fabric but often does. It enables branching lines or stems to be worked in a continuous process but gives a less distinct line than trailing. When worked loosely, in fine thread, it can give the appearance of a single, fine line to the naked eye.

Veined padded satin stitch - see **'Satin stitches'**.

Whipping A term most properly used for a technique in which an edge is loosely overcast and then the sewing thread is drawn up to gather the fabric but commonly used as an alternative to overcasting – see *'Whipped running'*.

Whitework/whitework embroidery Any embroidery in white thread on a white fabric.

Plate I.22 (left top) *The curls to the right of the image are in **trailing** but terminate in fronds of **whipped running** which is also used for the feathery stems to the left.*

Plate I.22a (left bottom) *The wrong side of the embroidery in Plate I.22. The overcasting stitches used in the 'trailing' all go through to the back of the fabric whereas the whipped stitches do not: the transparency of the fabric means that this does not show clearly.*

A few notes on the workers

At the beginning of the 19th century working practices had changed little from those used in the past. Embroidery was still purely a hand craft, worked by both amateurs and professionals. In Britain, Scotland had the greatest concentration of professional muslin workers, with thousands of women employed as 'flowerers' in the Ayrshire industry, but there were professionals working throughout the country. Some, such as the Moravians, lived in small communities, others worked as outworkers for individual retailers, such as haberdashers and milliners, some of the most skilled being employed by the specialist lace and embroidery merchants in London. Few details of pay and conditions are known but, despite its popularity and beauty, white embroidery was much less highly regarded and rewarded than work in expensive silk and metal threads, much of which was done by men.

On the amateur scene, whitework continued to be popular into the 1830s but, by this time, fashion required more complex patterns and stitching which were more time consuming and difficult to do. Also, by this time, a much simpler, quicker form of embroidery was becoming popular. This was 'Berlin wool-work', so-called for its use of woollen embroidery threads in vibrant colours imported from Berlin. A wide range of attractive artefacts from small costume accessories to household furnishings and pictures could be made by this technique and it soon superseded whitework as a pastime for those with time to spare for such crafts.

The basic production methods

The basic tools and techniques employed in the whitework industry in the 18th century continued in use through the 19th century and were described in some detail in our previous book. They will not, therefore, be dwelt on here at any length but, in brief:

- A master pattern would be drawn by a professional or amateur artist.
- Copies of the master pattern would be made by tracing : a copy would be used to transfer the pattern to the actual fabric to be worked or onto a stiff support, such as paper or parchment, on which a transparent material could be supported for working.
- The transfer from the copy could be effected either by pricking and pouncing directly onto the fabric or stiff support or by cutting a printing block and printing on the fabric with a washable ink.
- The embroidery would usually be worked with the fabric stretched, either tacked onto a support or mounted on a frame - either the drum-like tambour frame or a rectangular frame which could be small enough for home use or several yards long in a professional workshop.

A summary of changes in dominant embroidery stitches and design styles from the 1790s–1840s

The following guide to embroidery stitches and designs from the 1790s–1840s must not be taken as a set of definitive rules. It is impossible to pinpoint the earliest use of features that became dominant in later decades and early features rarely disappeared entirely. Thus all stitches in common use in the mid 18th century were used throughout the first half of the 19th century even though some were rare in early decades, while earlier design styles continued or were revived later on. Stitch and design alone, therefore, can give only a rough date for an article: for more precise dating the type and shape of the article on which they are used must also be considered.

The following summary applies specifically, though not exclusively, to accessories. Work on larger articles, such as household articles and complete dresses, was often of a heavier quality, worked in coarser threads and even in different styles.

1790s –1810s

Stitching and designs are generally simple, worked in very fine lines, but are quite varied stylistically.

Stitches

Motifs Satin stitch gradually gives way to padded satin stitch as the dominant stitch; it is worked in tiny or narrow areas
Lines In trailing, tambouring or whipped running, with tambouring going out of favour by the 1810s
Edges Straight (selvedge or very narrow hem) or lightly buttonholed in slight scallops; some vandyking
Other Little use of other stitches except overcast eyelets and lines of drawn or pulled work; some small areas of repetitive fillings

Designs

Mainly confined to narrow borders: a major proportion of fabric is plain or occasionally spotted.

- Sinuous trailing stems carrying tiny leaves or florets; repeated tiny, separate (discrete) motifs; neo-classical designs; some rococo-influenced motifs
- Lines are fine, usually single lines of stitching, while floral sprigs tend to be stiff

Plate I.23 (above) A neo-classical design from an apron including a repeated, largely symmetrical pattern of laurel wreaths, fountain-like sprays and swags within almost straight edges: mainly in satin stitch and whipped running: c1790-1810: Hereford M & AG, Cat. No. 5344.

Plate I.24 (left) A kerchief border and corner design including very simple, repetitive sprig motifs and a rococo floral spray with openwork fillings in the corner: mainly in satin stitch and whipped running inside a slightly scalloped, lightly buttonholed edge: c1790-1810: Walker M & AG, Cat. No.1963.287.65.

Plate I.25 (below) A sinuous flowering stem design for a border in padded satin stitch and trailing inside a slightly scalloped, buttonholed edge: from a long shawl; c.1800-15 - see Plate II.19. The denser, padded stitching gives much greater contrast with the ground than the satin stitch and whipped running in Plates I.23 and I.24.

Plate I.26 (above) Two simple, repetitive border designs of floral sprigs in padded satin stitch with overcast eyelets inside a more deeply scalloped, firmly buttonholed edge: c1810-20: from a kerchief - see Plate II.15.

LATE 1810s – LATE 1820s
Stitching and designs start to become more complex but are still largely confined to borders; floral designs predominate.

Stitches
Motifs Mainly tiny or narrow areas of padded satin stitch
Lines In trailing, whipped running: some linear designs in applied braid or tambouring
Edges Usually vandyked and buttonholed - either tiny points, or large points or scallops edged with tiny ones; some plain hems
Other Small areas of fillings become more common but repetitive; eyelets common

Designs
Mainly bold, floral and confined to borders.
- Repeated, separate, floral sprigs become progressively larger, often with distinct C-shaped curvature
- Floral trails mainly reserved for narrow outer borders
- Larger, asymmetric, discrete floral sprays are sometimes placed inside borders from the mid 1820s

Plate I.27 (above) Border from the pelerine in Plate II.91: mid-late 1820s. Each large point of the vandyked edge is cut into minute points and buttonholed. A discrete, curved, floral spray fills each large point inside a simple running design: in trailing and tiny areas of padded satin stitch with a repeated pulled-thread filling.

Plate I.28 (below) Corner of the pelerine in Plate II.82: mid-late 1820s. A large, discrete, asymmetric floral spray composed mainly of tiny areas of padded satin stitch sits inside a simple border and deep hem.

VERY LATE 1820s – MID 1830s
Designs mainly bold, floral and asymmetric, gradually becoming more spreading with a slightly greater variety of stitching: rococo influence gradually strengthens.

Stitches
Motifs Small, narrow areas of padded satin stitch: larger areas divided by clefts defining veins and indented edges become more and more common
- Trailed outlines introduced round padded satin stitch motifs in the 1830s
- Greater use of fillings but often repetitive

Lines In trailing or whipped running: some linear designs in applied braid or tambouring

Edges
- Vandyked (tiny points, or large points or scallops edged with tiny ones): buttonholed – simple form or transitional to scalloping, or
- Finished with a deep hem
- A narrow band of openwork bordered by trailed or buttonholed lines gradually becomes more common inside the actual edge

Other Appliqué work becomes more common

Designs
Mainly floral and asymmetric, gradually spreading from the borders and with contrast between bolder and lighter stitching gradually introduced in the 1830s.
- Discrete border sprigs gradually become more complex and, in the 1830s, spread into triangular forms often with S-curvature
- Border patterns often include a very simple narrow edge design outside a deeper band of decoration
- Large, discrete, isolated asymmetric sprays inside borders
- Patterned bands are formed by sinuous floral stems or discrete motifs which spread into each other in the 1830s
- Padded satin stitch motifs (particularly spots) with trailed outlines introduced by the mid 1830s
- Bold motifs are gradually contrasted with lighter, linear motifs including feathery fronds, branching and vermicular designs and coiling tendrils

Plate I.29 (left) Detail from the large triple pelerine in Plate II.131: early-mid 1830s.
The two deeply vandyked borders contain discrete floral sprays in the points and scallops inside a simple running design and edge of tiny buttonholed points: the bold sprays spread into roughly triangular shapes: in veined padded satin stitch and trailing with a few fronds in whipped running.

Plate I.32 (opposite bottom) Detail from the pelerine in Plate II.111: early-mid 1830s. The wide border design comprises two alternating floral sprays spreading, with S-shaped curvature, from a continuous floral trail. Bold components in trailing and padded satin stitch give some contrast with lighter, feathery fronds in whipped running. A narrow openwork band between two trailed lines runs inside the buttonholed, pointed edge.

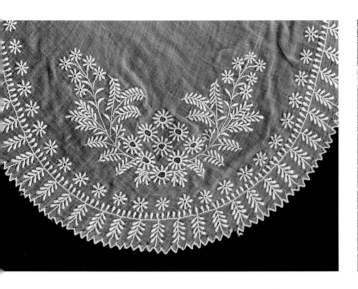

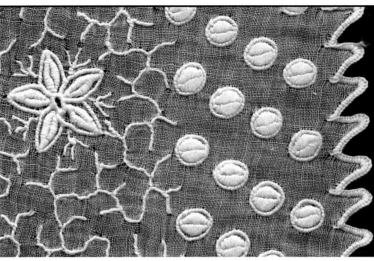

Plate I.30 (above) *Detail from the fichu pelerine in Plate II.107: early-mid 1830s. The edge is smoothly curved apart from tiny buttonholed points. A simple, repetitive, narrow border pattern follows the edge with a larger, spreading floral motif inside that: in trailing and padded satin stitch with needlepoint fillings in overcast eyelets.*

Plate I.31 (above) *Detail from the border of the pelerine in Plate II.162: c.mid 1830s. The bold padded satin stitch motifs have veins, or grooves, and trailed outlines and are contrasted with a lighter background of branching lines in whipped running.*

MID 1830s - EARLY 1840s
Designs mainly floral and rococo but cover larger areas;
a greater variety of styles and stitches introduced.

Stitches
Motifs Padded satin stitch often with clefts forming veins
and indented edges and/or trailed outlines
• Wider variety of stitches gradually introduced including
seeding, shadow work, sculpted areas of padded satin
stitch, eyelets and appliqué work
• Larger areas of openwork in a wider variety of filling
stitches
Lines Mainly in trailing or whipped running
• tambour work, particularly on larger articles
Edges In the mid 1830s still often vandyked and
buttonholed with scalloping more common
• Gently-curved edges gradually become more common;
smooth or with tiny buttonholed points
• Added lace or gathered muslin frills common
• A narrow band of openwork bordered by trailed or
buttonholed lines more common inside edges
• Wide bands of pulled- or drawn-thread work become
more common from the late 1830s

Designs
Rococo predominates but becomes mixed with a wide
variety of styles: often spread to cover whole articles.
• Mainly floral and asymmetric but other features gradually
introduced including: C- and S-shaped scrolls; cartouches
filled with varied filling stitches; arabesques; figural, diaper
and neo-classical motifs
• Long, roughly triangular sprays extend from borders
towards the centres of articles
• Borders include discrete motifs that spread into each other
gradually superseding continuous floral trails
• Contrast between bold motifs and lighter, linear
backgrounds first increases then gradually diminishes as
designs become filled with small motifs

*Plate I.33 (above) Detail from an 1830s rococo border including
spreading floral sprays with strong contrast between dense
components in padded satin stitch and feathery ones in whipped
running. Although discrete, the motifs almost merge with each other.
A narrow openwork band bordered by trailing runs inside the
buttonholed, pointed edge. From the pelerine in Plate II.151.*

Plate I.34 (above) Rococo corner design, late 1830s-early 1840s, including applied arabesques and other oriental shapes forming spaces for openwork fillings. The dense areas of appliqué work and padded satin stitch contrast with a background of feathery fronds in whipped running and a wide openwork border. From the triangular shawl in Plate II.240.

Plate I.35 (above left) Handkerchief corner with a fanciful design of a lion under a palm tree within a simple border: late 1830s. Different stitches create the varying textures of the lion.

Plate I.36 (opposite bottom) Detail from the fichu in Plate II.146: probably late 1830s. The smooth outline is edged with a narrow openwork band and bobbin lace trimming outside a narrow, almost continuous border of repeat floral sprays. Long sprays formed by a multitude of small flowers and leaves extend towards the centre. The previous strong contrast of bold motifs against a light background is lost in the mass of tiny motifs.

Plate I.37 (right bottom) Detail from the fichu in Plate II.225: early 1840s. The wide main panel has an all-over trellis, or diaper, design and a simpler outer border. The smoothly-curved edges are finished with a line of openwork and trimmed with bobbin lace; motifs are in padded satin stitch and seeding, with trailed lines.

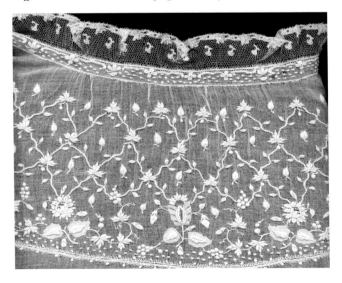

Section II

WHITE ACCESSORIES IN CONTEXT: HOW ACCESSORIES AND THEIR DESIGNS CHANGED TO COMPLEMENT THE EVER-CHANGING FASHIONS IN DRESS

A BRIEF OVERVIEW

We take up our story in the late18th century: white had become fashionable. Young and old alike might wear it from head to toe. Maids wore it as well as their mistresses. Only quality of fabric and decoration distinguished rich from poor and whitework embroidery, still entirely hand-worked, was one factor that made a difference. This scene could not last, of course. As the neo-classical influence waned, colour crept back into dress but this only increased the use of white accessories. These had not been quite as popular as implied above but, by the 1820s, they were coming back into their own. By the 1830s their use had exploded: embroidered pelerines, collars, canezous and shawls all contributed to the increasingly romantic, flamboyant and frivolous look of the period.

In the late 1830s the mood changed but fichus and capes that wrapped closely round the body could, in pure white, contribute to a more demure look. The popularity of whiteworked accessories was ensured.

GEORGE III ON THE THRONE

1789 FRENCH REVOLUTION

1791 BOSWELL'S LIFE OF JOHNSON; DEATH OF CHARLES WESLEY; MOZART'S DEATH AND 'REQUIEM'

1791-2 THOMAS PAINE'S 'THE RIGHTS OF MAN'

1793 EXECUTION OF LOUIS XVI OF FRANCE

1795 HAYDN'S 'LONDON' SYMPHONY

1796 JENNER'S FIRST COW-POX VACCINATION AGAINST SMALL POX

1798 NELSON WINS BATTLE OF THE NILE; FIRST STEAM-POWERED SPINNING MULE; HAYDN'S 'CREATION'; COLERIDGE'S 'RIME OF THE ANCIENT MARINER'

1799 NAPOLEON MADE FIRST CONSUL OF FRANCE

THE LATE 18TH CENTURY TO 1810s

During much of the 18th century, women wore long, full-skirted robes in coloured fabrics which the wealthy offset with fine white accessories, particularly kerchiefs, aprons and flowing sleeve ruffles, but by the 1780s fashions were changing. Excavations in Greece and Rome had awakened interest in the ancient world. Bleached statuary of women in flowing draperies sparked a desire for similar costumes and these could be made from the fine muslins more readily available due to the mechanisation of the textile trades and development of the American cotton plantations. The chemise dress, made in white muslin with a gathered bodice and soft skirt that fell gently to the ground, became popular initially for informal wear but gradually filtered into formal dress. The mood was one of romance and fantasy.

These changes, that had started gradually, were soon to become more rapid. In 1789, the upheaval that would bring Napoleon Buonaparte to power and war to the whole of Europe started with the French Revolution.

The 1790s were a time of turmoil and transition. Everything was in flux, the structure of Europe, of politics, of dress, of the decorative arts and of design.

In dress the changes came most rapidly at the end of the decade: skirts narrowed considerably while the waistline rose to give a wholly different silhouette. This, the neo-classical line, was one constant of the period: how it was achieved, the cut and construction of the gown, the shaping of bodice and neckline, varied enormously, as did the accessories.

The white or light-coloured dresses of the period were better complemented by coloured accessories but white was not entirely superseded. Decorative aprons still occasionally covered skirt fronts but were becoming less popular and, as sleeves lengthened, sleeve ruffles dwindled to a narrow frill at the wrist. The large kerchiefs known as buffons provided warmth around low necklines in the 1780s and continued in use through into the early 19th century despite the evidence of contemporary illustrations. The latter tended to show smaller kerchiefs tucked neatly into the neckline in the 1790s, draped more negligently in the 1800s or used to bind the curled hair in fashionably artistic arrangements: see Plates II.3 and II.4.

As the use of old accessories dwindled, new ones were introduced, particularly garments that compensated for the flimsiness of the dress itself. Long shawls and variously-shaped mantles with long lappets that fell almost to the hemline became popular to provide warmth while also enhancing the slim look of the fashion. These could be accompanied by habit shirts that took over the rôle of the kerchief in filling a low neckline.

All these accessories might be made in plain white muslin, or occasionally lawn. Plain, fine fabrics were fashionable as they had been at the very beginning of the 18th century but some decoration was acceptable: gathered ruffles were particularly popular, especially around low necklines, but also extended down the edges of any draped accessory. Patterns were usually confined to borders, with an occasional powdering of dots or sprigs over the ground, but the labour required to add this finery contributed to the exclusivity of the sheerest fabrics.

Plate II.1 (top right) Fashion Plate dated 1781 from a scrap album (Hereford M & AG) showing two women in open robes worn over petticoats visible at the front. The long, full skirts are typical of dress through most of the 18th century: only details such as the skirt shapes, the gathered flounces on one petticoat and the long sleeves suggest the late 18th century date. Both women wear white kerchiefs.

Kerchiefs

Having considered the general aspect of the period, we shall now come to specifics, looking first at the neck handkerchiefs, or kerchiefs, which continue the story of 18th-century dress. These might at the time be termed 'neckerchiefs' or, more usually, 'handkerchiefs', but I reserve that term for the later, smaller items intended to be carried in the hand and usually called 'pocket handkerchiefs'. The kerchief, as I shall call it,

Plate II.2 Fashion Plate dated 1785 from a scrap album (Hereford M & AG) showing a lady wearing a large kerchief, or buffon: the ends may be passed round her waist and fastened at the back.

Plate II.3 (above) *Fashion Plate of 1791 from a scrap album (Hereford M & AG) showing two seated ladies wearing round gowns (i.e. gowns closed at the front) with slimmer, more draped skirts than in Plate II.1 and waistlines defined by sashes. Both wear white kerchiefs; that on the left has a ruffled edge while that on the right is tucked neatly into the lady's low neckline.*

Plate II.4 (above) *Fashion Plate from the Ladies Magazine for December 1801 showing two ladies with 'dress kerchiefs' binding their hair to create a pseudo-classical look. Both kerchiefs have simple border patterns. One lady also has a coloured long shawl draped round her shoulders; coloured accessories were popular with the fashionable white robes of the period.*

was normally either a triangle of fabric or a square which was folded into a triangle for wear but the term was used loosely for other accessories worn around the neckline. When decorated, embroidered kerchiefs followed the contemporary fashions for added ruffles or minimalist patterns along the borders with, perhaps, additional corner motifs. Indeed the positioning and minimalism of design are the only clear points of reference for dating articles to the 1790s–early 1800s by their decoration. The neo-classical style that was the basis of dress also pervaded designs of the period but the earlier rococo style lingered on and repeated tiny, discrete floret and leaf designs developed. All of these can be seen in the following examples.

Starting with simplicity, the triangular kerchief in Plate II.5 is decorated solely with a ruffle along the central part of its longest edge while the other two edges are straight and bordered by dense, straight lines created in the weave. Straight edges or edges finished with very small, shallow scallops were the norm during this period.

Plates II.6 – II.16 show the variety of embroidery styles in vogue during the 1790s – 1810s, some in original examples, others in dated patterns. All of the designs could be adapted for use on kerchiefs or any of the other articles described below and all might have been used over many years, particularly by amateur embroiderers.

Plate II.5 *Triangular kerchief of fine muslin with a ruffle along the central part of its neck edge: c.1790-1810. Hereford M & AG Cat. No. 7350-4.*
The ruffle is beautifully gauged and whipped onto the rolled edge of the kerchief. The only other decoration consists of straight, narrow bands of slightly denser fabric created by the weave alongside the two shorter edges of the kerchief, one of which comprises the selvedge while the other is hemmed.
L long edge - 57in (145cm); L gathered ruffle - 28in (71cm); L short edges - 33in, 37in (84cm, 94cm); D ruffle - 2.5in (6.3cm)

Plate II.6a *A corner of the kerchief in Plate II.6.*
The outer edge is buttonholed in tiny, shallow scallops with a bobbin lace picot edging sewn on. Inside that is a row of discrete sprigs with tear-drop shaped leaves and an insertion of point-ground bobbin lace with a trail and sprig design (possibly English East Midlands work) held on each side by buttonhole stitches. Finally there are two rows of double-leaf sprigs.
The lace is folded to turn round two corners and cut on the diagonal on the other two corners. The embroidery is in satin stitch and trailing: the work is so neat that the two sides are almost identical.

Plate II.6 *A very large, square kerchief, or buffon, in extremely fine, supple muslin which drapes beautifully: c.1790-1800.*
Ls - 42in/42½in (106.5cm/107.5cm)
D pattern - 2¾in (7cm) including lace - 1⅛in (3cm)

Plate II.7 (right) *Pattern from 'The Ladies Magazine' of 1803 showing a 'New & Elegant Pattern for a Handkerchief or Apron'. The simplicity and repetition of the two alternating motifs in the border is typical of the period, as is the mix of classical symmetry with the asymmetry of the rococo. This type of design developed gradually from early-18th century patterns in which symmetrical corner motifs spread into bold, flowing borders patterned with numerous fillings but here the corner motif is reduced to an asymmetric spray and is separated from the simple border. Despite this, the old love of openwork fillings is catered for by the inclusion of filled racquet-like shapes but only one filling stitch is suggested.*

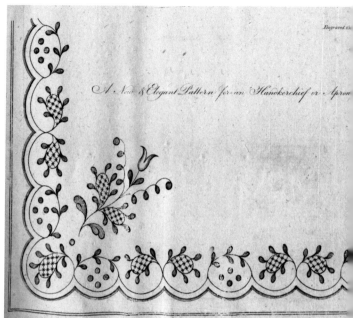

Plate II.8 (above) *A large square kerchief or buffon: c.1795-1810. This is clearly intended to be worn with one triangular half of the square turned over the other as the borders on two sides are much simpler than those on the others. Although not identical to the border design in Plate II.7, the main border bears a strong resemblance to it.*
Ls - 42in/41½in (106.5cm/105cm): D main border pattern - 1¾in (3.5cm) + lace - ½in (1.2cm)

Plate II.8a (right top left) *Detail of the kerchief in Plate II.8. The simpler border comprises a slightly scalloped, buttonholed edge with a wiggly tamboured line just inside it. These two lines continue along the other two edges where they border a design of repeated sprig motifs worked with tamboured lines, tiny satin-stitch leaves and a single pulled-thread filling.*
The fabric is cut away from the buttonholing on the simpler edges but the other two edges are finished with a straight, rolled hem to which a narrow point-ground bobbin lace border (probably English East Midlands work) is added.

Plates II.9a, b and c (right) *Three patterns from 'The Ladies Magazine' of 1803 each showing a 'New & Elegant Pattern for a Veil etc.'*
Being described as patterns for 'veils', these might be intended for working in lace or embroidered net but are equally suitable for whitework embroidery on muslin. All show a mix of classical and rococo features, some with small areas for fillings. All consist mainly of very fine lines carrying minute leaves and petals.

Plate II.10 'Original Pattern for the Collar of a Shirt & half Handkerchief in White or Col.d Silks in Tambour for N38 of La Belle Assemblée (Nov 1808)'

The lower design is clearly for the half handkerchief while the collar may be for a lady's shirt or habit shirt, of which more below.

Although designed for working with a tambour hook, these patterns could equally well be worked with a needle. Indeed this would probably be easier as the laurel sprigs do not actually touch to form a continuous chain which is easier for tambour work. The laurel sprigs and spots are absolutely typical of designs of the period, laurel in particular being associated with the classical repertoire. The long shawl shown in Plates II.16, II.16a has a very similar design.

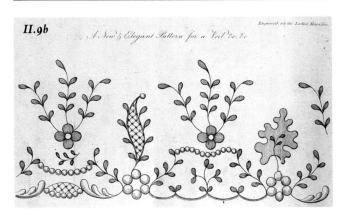

Most of the designs in Plates II.6–II.16 are confined to narrow borders but that in Plate II.11 is more complex, with neo-classical, fountain-like sprays spreading into the spotted ground. The whole pattern is, however, still composed of a multitude of tiny, discrete areas and narrow lines and the whole border would occupy a relatively small area of the finished handkerchief. It is therefore fully in accord with the taste of its period.

In practice, such complex designs are seen more often on surviving dresses than on smaller articles but fairly similar handkerchiefs or veils are seen in the fashion illustration in Plate II.12. Here they are worn draped in various ways over the head.

Plate II.12 (above) Detail from a fashion illustration of February 1805 showing 'London Head Dresses'. Several of the head dresses include white articles draped in various manners. These could be of lace rather than whitework but the designs of leafy floral sprays in corners or along edges are similar to that in Plate II.11.

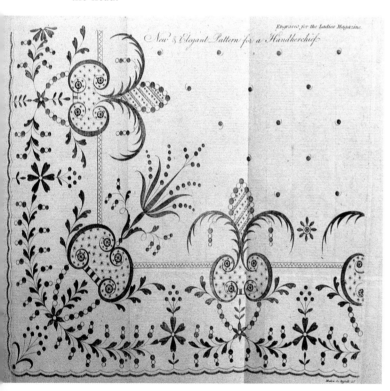

Plate II.11 (above) Embroidery pattern for a handkerchief from the 'Ladies Magazine' of 1805: Exeter University Library.

Plate II.13 (right) Portrait of Lady Mountnorris with a handkerchief draped over her head: from the Fashion Magazine 'La Belle Assemblée' of 1811.
The fashion for wearing kerchiefs over the head started in the late 18th century and, as we see here, was still present in the 1810s, worn as an alternative to a day cap.

The kerchiefs shown in Plates II.6 and II.8 are complete squares but half handkerchiefs were still in use. Like the 18th century versions, their longer sides could be plain but, at least from the early 19th century, examples are found with patterning on all three sides. The pattern in Plate II.14 is for such a kerchief and makes use of the 'Greek key' motif, another favourite classical design. The surviving example in Plate II.15, on the other hand, has borders of simple sprigs formed by overcast eyelets and tiny leaf shapes worked in padded satin stitch. The latter gives much greater contrast with the fine muslin ground than the simple satin stitch seen previously: it came to dominate whitework embroideries in the early 19th century.

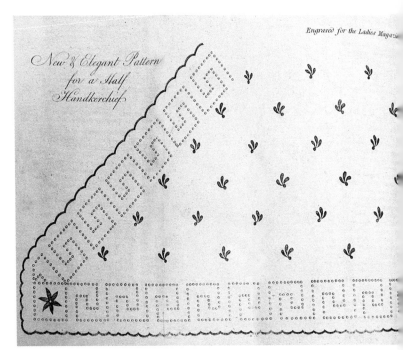

Plate II.14 (above right) Pattern from the 'Ladies Magazine' of 1805 showing a 'New & Elegant Pattern for a Half Handkerchief'. This classical Greek key pattern would be worked along all three edges inside a slightly scalloped border. The ground is spotted with tiny leafy sprigs.

Plate II.15 (left) Triangular kerchief: probably 1810s.
The kerchief is finished on all three edges with tiny buttonholed scallops and narrow border designs leaving a large area of plain ground in the centre. The complex scallops of the longer edge are occupied by very simple, upright florets each comprising an overcast eyelet and two padded satin stitch leaves carried on a short stem. The scallops of the shorter borders are simpler but the pattern of discrete florets bending towards the edge is bolder. For a detail see Plate I.26, p21.
Ls - approx. 38in (96.5cm)

1800 BEETHOVEN'S 1ST SYMPHONY

1805 BATTLE OF TRAFALGAR; NELSON'S DEATH

1806-7 ABOLITION OF THE SLAVE TRADE

1808-09 HEATHCOAT PATENTED MACHINES FOR MAKING A STABLE NET COPYING THE 'POINT GROUND' NET OF EAST MIDLANDS BOBBIN LACES

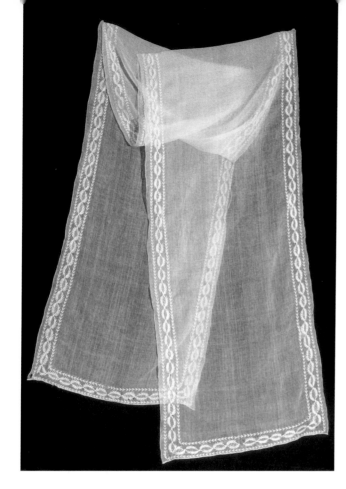

Plate II.16 A long shawl in very fine, soft muslin with a narrow whiteworked border: late 1790s-early 1810s.
The laurel-trail design is almost identical to that shown for a half handkerchief in Plate II.10. L - 111in (282cm); W - 19in (48cm) D border - 2¼in (5.5cm) on sides, 1¾in (4.5cm) at ends

enhance the desired tall, elegant line of the body and the sense of flowing drapery achieved by the lightweight dress fabrics. At the same time, they provided warmth and their floral patterns added a touch of colour.

The Kashmiri products became so popular that their designs were taken up by our own industries and started a gradually evolving story that continued through into the late 19th century. So many shawls were made in Paisley that a stylised version of the boteh even came to be known in Britain as the 'Paisley pattern'.

Although many of the long shawls worn in the 1790s to 1810s were in bright colours to provide a contrast to pale or white dresses (see Plate II.4), white, particularly in diaphanous muslin, was also fashionable. Eventually, as we shall see, the Kashmiri designs were copied in whitework but the few surviving whiteworked shawls that I have found from the 1790s to 1810 are worked in the European designs already seen in kerchiefs. They do, however, have some features in common with their Kashmiri counterparts: designs consist of very narrow border patterns all round with any additional patterning being confined to the ends apart from occasional sprigged centres. Several examples and fashion illustrations are shown in Plates II.16-II.28.

The first shawl (Plates II.16, 16a) is very long (9ft 3in -282cm) and narrow (19in - 48cm), giving proportions which, together with its very simple border design, would make it look similar to the shawl illustrated in Plate II.17 in wear: the proportions are a useful indication of an early date although wider shawls were also worn in this period (see Plate II.18). The border pattern of intertwined laurel trails sandwiched between straight trails is typically neo-classical although the 18th-century liking for openwork fillings is still apparent in the inclusion of pulled-thread work in spaces defined by the trails. Jane Austen worked a shawl of similar proportions to the

Shawls

By the late 18th century kerchiefs were being accompanied or superseded by various mantles, scarves and shawls for wear round the shoulders, the names being by no means standardised. Our word 'shawl' in fact derives from the Persian word 'schal' used for the lengths of Kashmiri goat-hair (cashmere) fabrics imported by the British East India Company. The early shawls had narrow floral borders all round and short end panels worked with repeated floral sprays known as 'buta' or 'boteh': the centres might be plain or, more rarely, filled with organised rows of floral sprigs. The lightness, suppleness and length of these shawls made them particularly suitable for wear with the neo-classical style of dress as they could be draped from the shoulders to

shawl in Plate II.16 but with a trellis design including four-petalled flowers in padded satin stitch at each corner instead of the laurel trail. It has no openwork fillings but the flowers are repeated in a spot pattern across the centre. It still survives at Jane's home, Chawton House, at Alton.

The shawl shown in Plate II.19 also has similar proportions and is made in an even finer, almost transparent muslin. Its design and stitching are more characteristic of the early 19th century than the late 18th century. The embroidery, mainly in heavily padded satin stitch, must have appeared to float on air when worn.

Plate II.18 (right) *Detail from a fashion illustration from* La Belle Assemblée *for August 1806 showing a lady wearing a wide shawl draped around her shoulders. The outfit is more suited to the British climate than that in Plate II.17.* *(Harris M & AG)*

Plate II.16a (above) *Detail of the shawl in Plate II.16. The heavily-padded satin stitch makes a strong contrast with the semi-transparent ground while the filling stitches between the intertwined trails are so fine as to be scarcely visible. The long edges comprise the selvedges of the fabric while the ends are hemmed. A tear near the corner is beautifully darned, a common feature of old accessories: fine fabric and embroidery were far too precious to throw away if they could be repaired.*

Plate II.17 (right) *Illustration of 'Parisian Costume' for the year 1797. The lady seen here is in a far more scanty, transparent gown than is likely to have been seen in Britain at the time but, over it, she wears a long shawl (Schall Long) that would have been perfectly acceptable. An example of similar transparency is seen in Plate II.19.*

Plate II.19a (above) Detail of the long shawl in Plate II.19. The border comprises a sinuous, leafy stem from which flower heads spread into the spaces on opposite sides between lines of drawn-thread work. The motifs consist entirely of elongate shapes of padded satin stitch which is also used for wider lines in the design, narrower lines being trailed. The lightly scalloped edge is buttonholed. See Plate I.25 for closer detail.

Plate II.20a (below) A detail of an end panel of the shawl in Plate II.20. The lines are worked in whipped running stitch, the leaves in satin stitch: these contrast far less with the muslin ground than the padded satin stitch of the shawl in Plates II.19, II.19a.

Plate II.19 (above) A long shawl of almost transparent muslin with a simple running border pattern and a sprig motif in each corner; c.1800-1815. The embroidery is so neat that it is effectively double-sided. The stiff, rather simple nature of the corner sprigs is typical of the very early 19th century.
L - 103in (261cm); W - 16in (40cm); D border - 2in (5cm).

In addition to long, rectangular shawls, many variations on the theme were available including ones with shaped ends and gathered frills. One such shawl can be seen in our book on 18th century whitework: another is shown in Plates II.20, II.20a. This is essentially a long rectangle that is cut away in the centre of one long edge to fit neatly round the neckline in wear as demonstrated by the lady on the left in Plate II.21. The pattern of the shawl bears comparison with the handkerchief pattern of 1805 in Plate II.11 although it is rather slighter in character suggesting an earlier date, commensurate with the fashions of 1799 in Plate II.21.

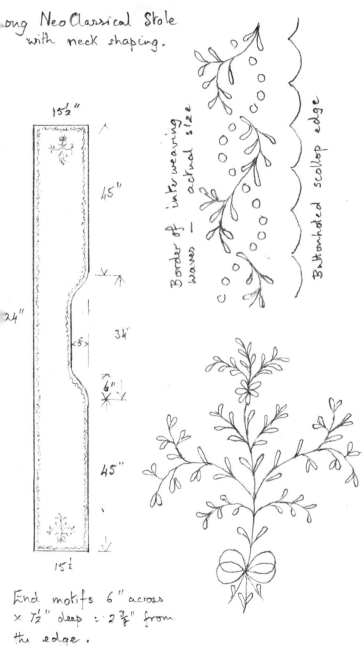

ong NeoClassical Stole
with neck shaping.

15½"

45"

24"

‹5›

3½"

6"

45"

15½"

Border of lines wearing waves – actual size

Buttonholed scallop edge

End motifs 6" across
× 7½" deep : 2⅜" from
the edge.

Plate II.21 (right)
*Fashion Illustration
from a scrap album
(Hereford M & AG)
showing walking dresses of
1799. Both ladies wear
light-coloured robes with
trailing skirts. The long
blue shawl worn by
the lady on the left
has a shaped
neckline like that
in Plate II.20.
The lady on
the right
wears an over-
garment with
similar long
lappets falling
down the front
but attached to a yoke
and a standing collar.
The outfits are obviously
intended for winter wear as
they include large muffs
which were particularly
fashionable at the turn of
the 19th century.*

Plate II.20 (left) *Drawing of a shawl or mantle comprising a long
rectangle of fabric with the central portion of one edge cut away: late
1790s-early 1800s. Worthing M & AG; Cat. No.61/715
A simple running border of leaf sprays intertwined with lines of dots
surrounds the entire article while each end is also embroidered with a
single, large, spindly, fountain-like spray with a double-bow at its base.*

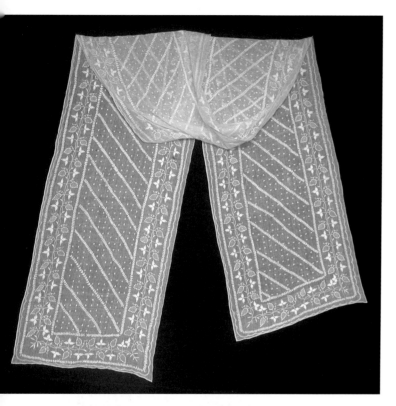

A further shawl is shown in Plates II.22-II.22c. Here the border, though simple, takes up a slightly greater proportion of the whole than in previous examples and the centre is filled with diagonal bands of leafy trails and a spot pattern. The border pattern bears a marked resemblance to a dated pattern of 1810 (Plate II.23) but the central design echoes the banding of a dress of about 1815-20 shown in Plate II.24: diagonally-banded fabric was particularly popular in the late 1810s to1820s although earlier examples are known. Such overlaps of design trends were very common and add to the difficulty of dating accessories such as these.

A further complication in dating lies in the type of embroidery employed: most of the trails and dense pattern areas in this shawl are worked in whipped running which does not contrast so sharply with the ground as the padded satin stitch of the shawls in Plates II.16 and II.19. Whipped running was more common in 18th-century than 19th-century work but is far less time consuming to do than padded satin stitch and, in view of the area of this shawl covered with embroidery, the use of quicker stitching is readily understandable.

Plate II.22 (top) *A long shawl of diaphanous muslin with a wide trailing border pattern confined by two narrow straight trails and a centre filled with diagonal trails and spots; probably c.1810-1820. Diagonal banding is seen in the dress fabric of the robe in Plate II.24. L - 108in (274cm); W - 25in (64cm); D border pattern - 2in (5cm)*

Plate II.22a (left) *A corner of the long shawl in Plate II.22. The long edges are selvedges: the short edges have rolled hems. A scalloped line of chain stitch bordered by smaller buttonholed scallops runs just inside all the edges.*

Plate. II.23 (above) *Border patterns of 1810*

Plate II.24 (right) *A robe from the Devonshire collection shown with a long shawl of diaphanous muslin with a design imitating that of early 19th-century Kashmiri shawls: see Plates II.28, 28a for details. The dress fabric is printed with wavy diagonal bands in white, mauve and a darker stripe but these are overlaid by stronger vertical stripes. Similar diagonal banding occupies the centre of the shawl in Plate II.22.*

Plate II.22b (bottom left) *Closer detail of the shawl in Plate II.22. The embroidery is worked in a fairly thick, soft thread mainly in whipped running with pulled-thread fillings.*

> **1811-20** TRUE REGENCY PERIOD (GEORGE, LATER GEORGE IV, WAS REGENT FOR HIS FATHER GEORGE III); FIRST GAS STREET LIGHTING; LUDDITE MOVEMENT DESTROYS MECHANISED KNITTING FRAMES IN NOTTINGHAM AND LATER POWERED LOOMS FURTHER NORTH; JANE AUSTEN'S WORKS PUBLISHED
>
> **1814-32** SIR WALTER SCOTT'S NOVELS
>
> **1815** BATTLE OF WATERLOO
>
> **1816** ROSSINI'S 'BARBER OF SEVILLE'
>
> **1818** MARY SHELLEY'S 'FRANKENSTEIN'

It has already been mentioned that the word 'shawl' came into our language with the importation of Kashmiri 'schal' goods in the late 18th century. One such shawl is carried by the lady in Plate II.25 with a similar one being worn by the lady in Plate II.26. The illustrations are dated 1819 and 1822 respectively and show a very restrained, early form of the boteh design despite the fact that more complex designs had developed by the 1820s. Plate II.27 shows a detail from an end panel of an early 19th century shawl with a typical boteh design.

Given the popularity of such shawls it is not surprising that whitework copies were made but I have seen none that I would date to the earliest period of importation, that is, the late 18th century. Examples with designs similar to those shown in Plates II.25 and II.26, however, appear to be relatively common. One is shown in wear in Plate II.24, with details in Plates II.28, II.28a.

Whiteworked shawls with this simple design format occur in various widths and, despite their early form, some may date from later in the 19th century, particularly the 1840s.

I have seen none with designs matching the complexity of later Paisley shawls and other coloured equivalents.

Plate II.25 (left) *Parisian fashion for 1819 showing a lady wearing a walking outfit comprising a blue 'Redingote de gros de Naples' with a Kashmiri-style shawl draped over one arm. One end panel of the shawl is clearly visible: it has a boteh design bordered by narrow patterned bands. The central mass of the shawl is plain. The lady also wears a white ruff which might be of lace or whitework and a satin bonnet with a lace veil.*

Plate II.26 (right) *Fashion illustration of 1822. The lady's height and length of her Kashmir shawl are rather exaggerated but give a good idea of the proportions of the shawl design: the patterning is mainly at the ends where repeated, discrete, floral motifs are confined between a narrow floral band that surrounds the entire shawl (not all visible) and a similar band that partitions them from the plain centre.*

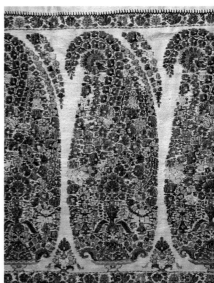

Plate II.27 (top right) Detail from an early 19th century woven long shawl showing part of the decorative end panel. This shawl, which is of European manufacture imitating contemporary Kashmir shawls, is typical of the early 19th century style. Each boteh motif includes a base or shallow vase which supports massed flower heads arranged in the shape of a pine cone with a tip curved over to one side. There is no outline to the boteh as there is in later designs. Slight floral motifs occupy but do not fill the gaps between the boteh.

Plate II.28 (top left) End panel from the long shawl in Plate II.24 showing typical whiteworked boteh motifs. The organisation of the design and the proportions of the shawl are similar to those of the shawls shown in Plates II.25-II.27. The only obvious difference is that the centre of this whitework shawl is filled with dots.

Plate II.28a (bottom right) Closer detail of the long shawl in Plate II.28 showing the dense padded satin stitch used for the motifs: the stems are in trailing and whipped running while the dots in the ground comprise buttonholed eyelets. Despite the overall size of the boteh motifs, the design is worked in tiny areas of padded satin stitch like other whitework designs of the period.

The boteh motif is something of an anomaly in our whitework story: although seen on shawls, it does not appear to have become popular on other accessories until about the middle of the 19th century and then only in a simplified form. The asymmetric, curving floral nature of the boteh, however, probably did influence the development of floral motifs that came to dominate designs from the late 1810s into the 1830s. We shall see these later on but, to complete the story of accessories at the beginning of our period, we must return to the 1780s and the development of the habit shirt.

The habit shirt, shirt handkerchief or chemisette

As its name implies, the habit shirt, often simply referred to as a shirt, was initially similar to a man's shirt and was developed for wear under a riding habit: the lady in the riding habit in Plate II.29 probably wears such a shirt. It has ruffles down the front opening like those being attached to the man's shirt in Plate II.30. At what date the full shirt was simplified to the form now commonly understood as the 'habit shirt' is unclear but at some stage the sleeves were omitted and the side bodice seams left open. Our first example, shown in Plates II.31-31c, is probably not from the very earliest period but is illustrative of the early style. It is made of linen and has a surprisingly complex structure. It is front-opening, with two square front panels, a deep standing band, or collar, a triangular back panel and triangular insets on the shoulders similar to those of men's shirts of the period. The front panels are beautifully gauged for attachment to the collar and shoulder inserts while the back panel is ungathered. There is no whitework

Plate II.29 Fashion Illustration dated 1783 from a scrap album (Hereford M & AG) showing a lady wearing a red riding habit over a white undergarment, either a shirt or habit shirt. This has a high standing collar and gathered frills down the front opening like those of a man's shirt. The habit sleeves are long and tight but narrow white ruffles show at the wrists. These may be part of the shirt or may be attached to separate bands tacked into the cuffs of the riding habit.

embroidery but plain frills are gauged and whipped to the front edges of the front panels and to the free edge of the collar, the upper part of which would have been turned down in wear. The very shallow depth of the back panel, even with the addition of a tape loop for fastening it, suggests a date for this habit shirt in the very late 1790s–1810s, in keeping with the high waistlines of dress during this period.

Another habit shirt of about the same period is shown in Plate II.32. This looks superficially like that in Plate II.31 but has a much deeper triangular back panel and lacks the latter's complex structure: it may be of earlier or later date.

Plate II.30 *A print from 'Le Bon Genre' of about 1817 entitled 'Le Vieux jeune homme'.*
The scene shows a shop assistant attempting to pin a ready-made shirt ruffle to a gentleman's shirt under his admiring gaze. Another assistant holds a ruffle taken from a pile on the counter while yet another carries out some sewing: a more senior woman makes notes in a book. All women wear different forms of ruffled neckwear and caps, demonstrating the ubiquity of ruffled decoration in the period as well as its commercial manufacture.
Shirt ruffles were often of a finer fabric than the shirt body and might be sewn up with the shirt or made up separately, as here. Separate ruffles could easily be removed for laundering. The man also wears a cravat tied in a bow around his high standing collar.

Linen Habit Shirt

II.31

Actual Size of
gusset and
overlaid
band

gummy edge concealed inside
the collar

back stitched through all layers

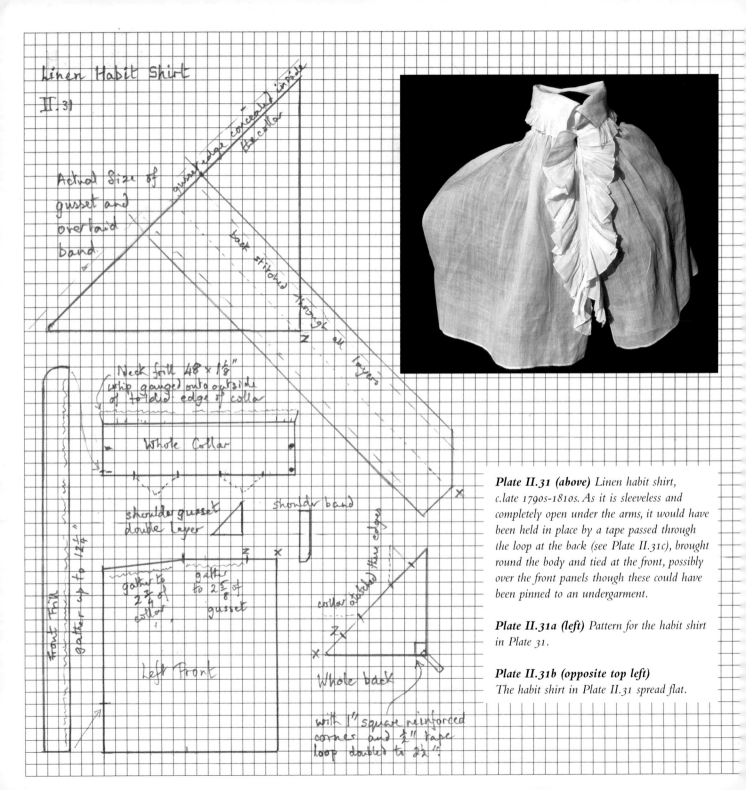

Neck frill 48 × 1⅛"
(whip gauged) onto outside
of folded edge of collar

Whole Collar

shoulder gusset
double layer

shoulder band

Front frill

gather up to 12¼"

gather to
2¾ of
collar

gather
to 2⅝ of
gusset

collar extends thru edges

Left Front

Z

Whole back

with 1" square reinforced
corners and ¾" tape
loop doubled to 2½"

Plate II.31 (above) *Linen habit shirt,
c.late 1790s-1810s. As it is sleeveless and
completely open under the arms, it would have
been held in place by a tape passed through
the loop at the back (see Plate II.31c), brought
round the body and tied at the front, possibly
over the front panels though these could have
been pinned to an undergarment.*

Plate II.31a (left) *Pattern for the habit shirt
in Plate 31.*

Plate II.31b (opposite top left)
The habit shirt in Plate II.31 spread flat.

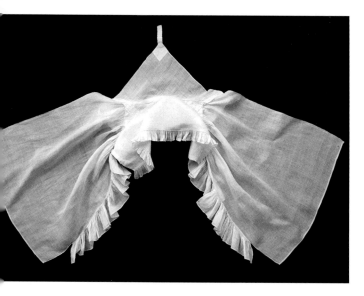

Plate II.31c (top right) *Detail of the habit shirt in Plate II.31.*
Part of the upper edge of each front panel is gauged and caught
between the two layers of the collar and a triangular inset, or gusset,
on the shoulder: the frills are whipped to the collar and front panels.
The two mother-of-pearl buttons and corresponding button holes are
the only front fastenings. A tape is sewn inside the front edge of the
collar to support the buttons.

Plate II.32 (bottom right) *Linen habit shirt: 1790s/1820s?*
The front and back panels are seamed at the shoulders but without
the triangular inserts of the shirt in Plate II.31. The front neck
edges are gauged and caught between the two layers of the standing
collar while the back edges are simply gathered. The deep triangular
back panel suggests a date when waistlines were lower, either the
1790s or 1820s. The front ruffles are decorated with single tucks
alongside, and of the same width as, their hems (⅛in - 3mm):
a separate neck ruffle might have been worn.
Front panels - D - 16in (40.6cm); W - 14¼in (36.5cm)
Back panel (cut on the cross) - CB - 15¾in (40cm)
Shoulder seam - 7½in (19cm): Collar - D - 2⅞in (7.3cm);
L - 13¾in (35cm): D ruffles - 1¾in (4.5cm)

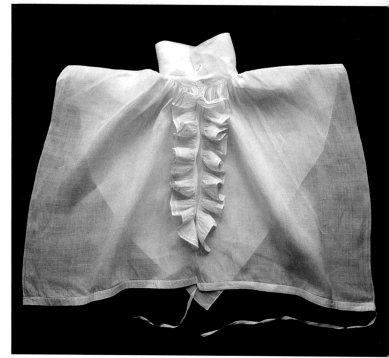

Plate II.33 (top left) *Back-opening habit shirt: c1800 – 1820. This is cut in one piece with the pin-tucked front panels on the straight and the back panels on the cross. It fastens by means of three decorated Dorset buttons on the collar and five down the back. The gauging of the neck frill to the collar shows that it was intended to turn down rather than up.*

Habit shirts suitable for wear with riding habits continued in use through the first half of the 19th century but, once established as a convenient garment, variations soon developed and were also used with other forms of dress. Plate II.33, for example, shows a very much simpler version with a back opening and pin-tucked decoration down the front. This, like many habit shirts and later chemisettes, is made of a firmer fabric than muslin: added frills, or ruffles, were commonly of finer fabric than the main body of such garments.

Plate II.34 shows how such a habit shirt might look when worn, with one difference: the illustration shows a double rather than a single neck ruffle. Single, double and triple forms were common: they could be sewn to the neckband of a habit shirt or to that of a dress or other garment or to a totally separate neckband. The Platt Hall collection, Manchester, holds many such ruffles, or ruffs, each comprising a neck band carrying one, two or three fine muslin frills: all are undecorated but their fine gauging would have required much skill and patience. A similar ruff dating from about the 1820s from its embroidery style is shown in Plates II.63-63b.

Plate II.34 (bottom left) *Detail from a fashion illustration showing Parisian dress from 'The Lady's Magazine' of July 1803. The lady's dark blue robe, probably a riding habit, is worn over a back-opening white undergarment, probably a habit shirt. The front panel is gathered or tucked with vertical tucks and attached to a standing band which carries a double ruffle.*

Another early habit shirt is shown in Plates II.35, 35a. This is decorated with applied braids placed so as to resemble frogging on military uniforms, a common feature of female dress during times of war when officers were frequently seen in uniform in public. During the early years of the century Britain was, of course, at war with Napoleonic France.

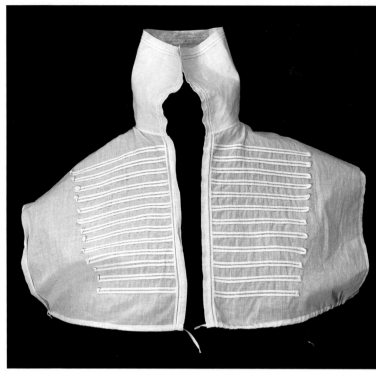

Plate II.35 (right) Front-opening habit shirt: about 1800-1815: Hereford M & AG, Cat. No. 2356.
The horizontal bands of applied braid resemble the decoration on military uniforms of the period. The extremely high standing collar would probably have been worn with the front corners turned down like that worn by the lady on the left in Plate II.36.
(See next page for detail)
CF - 8¾in (22.3cm); CB - 9¾in (24.8cm); D collar - 4½in (11.5cm); L collar - 15in (43cm); W braid - ⅛in (0.3cm)

Plate II.36 (left) Fashion illustration dated 1802 from a scrap album in the Hereford M & AG.
The lady, left, appears to be wearing a dress cut extremely low on the bosom but with the neckline filled with a habit shirt with an extremely high standing collar. Its corners are turned down under her chin in the manner of a man's collar of the period.
The central lady has a white frill close under her chin but the coloured kerchief around her neck makes it impossible to see whether this is part of her dress or a habit shirt, or is a separate accessory.
The lady, right, has a white collar, probably part of her dress, turned over the collar of her dark blue jacket, or spencer.

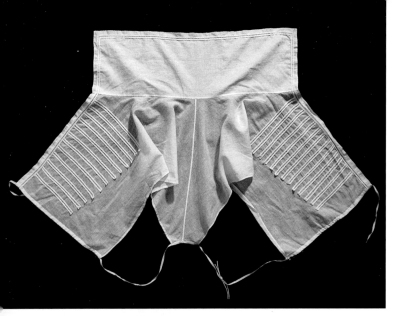

Returning to the ubiquitous ruffles of the period, the lady in Plate II.37 wears an outfit with a plunging neckline, itself finished with a frill but also partly filled by an additional layer of fabric with a frill along its upper edge: this may be the neckline of a habit shirt or simply that of a small panel of fabric, later called a modesty piece, which might be pinned in place to hide the décolletage (later examples are shown in Plates II.177-179). A separate neck ruff, comprising a band with ruffles along its upper and lower edges, is also worn.

Examples of habit shirts with lower necklines are shown in Plates II.38 and II.39. The latter can be dated generally to the early 19th century by its extremely shallow body but waistlines were high for a considerable period, from the late 1790s to the early 1820s, so that close dating is unsafe. Habit shirts, later called chemisettes, with similar ruffled necklines can also be seen in fashion illustrations as late as the 1840s: only the depth of the chemisette body may indicate the date of a surviving example.

Plate II.35a (above) The habit shirt in Plate II.35 laid flat. The body is cut in two pieces joined at a centre-back seam; the centre backs are on the cross, the fronts on the straight grain of the fabric. A waist tape passes through casings at the lower edges of the front and back panels.

Plate II.37 (left) Fashion Plate of about 1799 from the Hampshire collection showing a lady in a robe with a low-necked, high-waisted bodice worn beneath an over-robe with an even lower neckline.
A small panel of fabric, possibly a 'modesty piece', with a gathered frill partly fills the décolletage while a neckband carrying narrow, gathered ruffles along its upper and lower edges encircles the neck.

Plate II.38 (right) Detail from a fashion illustration of 1807.
The plain, low neckline of the lady's white robe is filled with a habit shirt, or chemisette, with a neck frill. Typically the white robe is offset by a coloured outer garment and bonnet.

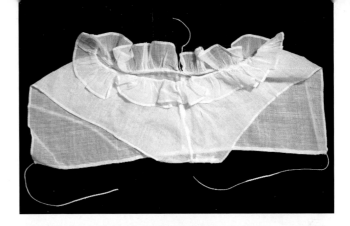

Plate II.39 Habit shirt, or chemisette, with a low neckline and gauged neck frill (seen from the back): c1800-1820: Worthing M & AG, Cat. No.X/1964/1052.

The body of the habit shirt is formed from two pieces of plain cotton fabric seamed together down the centre front and centre back to form the rectangular front panel and truncated-triangular back panel: the fronts are on the straight grain of the fabric, the backs on the cross. The shirt has no front opening, being designed to be put on over the head. In addition to the frill, the neckline is formed with a casing which houses a draw string on which it could be gathered to look like the habit shirt in Plate II.38.

CF - 5in (13cm); CB - 5¾in (15cm); D frill - 2in (5cm)

Some idea of the varied cut, construction and wear of habit shirts of the period will have been gained from the examples above but, to return to the question of decoration, two embroidered examples are next shown together with printed embroidery patterns. The first (Plates II.40-II.40b) comprises a single rectangle of fine muslin with a circular hole cut for the neck and a slit for a back opening: a standing collar with a small recess in its upper edge is seamed to the neck edge with the recess at the front. The embroidery on the main, front panel is in the same positions as that shown in a printed pattern of 1805 (Plate II.41) and, although not identical in design, is perfectly appropriate for an early 19th century date. The pattern indicates that this might have been called a 'shirt handkerchief' at the time.

Plate II.40 A habit shirt, or shirt handkerchief, cut from a rectangular panel of muslin with an added standing collar: Hereford M & AG, Cat. No.5427.

The cut edges of the back opening are hemmed and four Dorset buttons are added to one side with corresponding button holes on the other. (See next page for details)

W - 15¾in (40cm); L - 23in (58.5cm); CF - 10¾in (27.3cm); CB - 6½in (16.5cm); W neck - 5½in (14cm): Collar - L - 14½in (36.8cm); D - 3in (7.6cm): W Embroidery - 10½in (26.7cm)

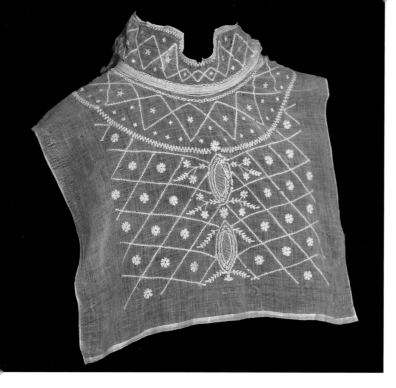

Plate II.40b (below) *A detail of the habit shirt in Plate II.40. The diaper lines and tiny flower heads are worked in chain stitch, probably tamboured, while stronger lines are worked in stitches drawn tight to create holes. Pulled-thread work fills the two central leaf shapes.*

Plate II.40a (above) *The habit shirt in Plate II.40 arranged as in wear to show the standing collar more clearly*

Plate II.41 (left) *Pattern dated 1805 'for a shirt handkerchief' showing the dual use of the terms 'shirt' and 'handkerchief' at the time (Exeter University Library).*
Although the major panels of accessories and garments in this period were, for the most part, decorated only along the borders, with perhaps a narrow band down the front of a dress, bodices and sleeves might be fully patterned. The arrangement of the pattern here, in bands of different designs, is typical of the period. Often such panels were made from bands of different fabrics such as whitework and lace.

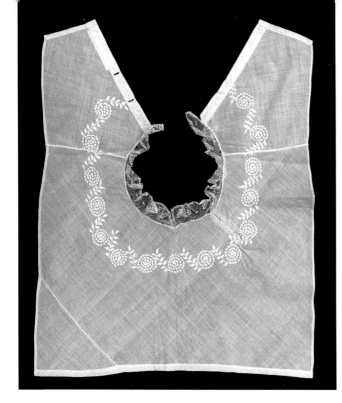

Plate II.42 (above) *Habit shirt, or shirt handkerchief, made from four pieces of fabric with embroidery worked across the shoulder seams. All of the pieces are cut on the cross. (Harris M & AG)*

Plate II.42a (top right) *Detail of the habit shirt in Plate II.42. The embroidery is in satin stitch, the frill in point-ground bobbin lace, probably of East Midlands manufacture. The design is also shown in Plate II.43.*

The second embroidered example (Plates II.42, 42a) is simpler than the first in that it has only a single band of embroidery round the neck and a bobbin lace frill instead of the standing collar. What is interesting is that it has two back panels and a composite front panel. Clearly the maker has made use of fragments of material: fine fabrics like this were far too expensive to waste. A further point of interest is that the embroidery design is identical to that in a printed pattern of 1808 (Plate 43) except for the fact that the latter is for a corner motif rather than a circular band.

Plate II.43 (below) *Embroidery pattern dated 1808 (Exeter University Library). The two patterns, though stated as being for 'shirt handkerchiefs', are clearly for what we might describe as 'kerchief corners': terminology was not consistent at the time, making it difficult for us to interpret written documentary evidence. One pattern comprises neo-classical scrolls of dots alternating with, and linked by, laurel sprays: the other has a very different, floral character. Its leafy trail is, however, similar to that in the 1805 design (Plate II.41): only the larger leaf spray in the corner gives the design a fuller appearance.*

Plate II.44 *Fashion illustration from La Belle Assemblée for 1806 (Harris M & AG).*

One lady (right) holds the edge of a voluminous white apron and wears a triangular white kerchief thrown loosely round her shoulders. The apron appears to be caught under a waist belt and may also have a bib like those shown in Plates II.49, II.50. It has a pleated or gathered ruffle along three sides: although difficult to discern, the ruffle is patterned with six-petalled flower heads while larger, similar flower heads form an inner border. This apron, like others shown here, is purely decorative, unlike the plain, black apron worn by the shop assistant in Plate II.30

The lady on the left has a long shawl with a very narrow decorative border draped over the back of her chair.

Aprons

It has already been said that whiteworked aprons did not have the importance in the 19th century that they had had in the 18th century. Indeed, comparatively few survive or are seen in illustrations but a statement from a fashion magazine of 1805 reads '...in an adjusted undress an apron of fine muslin, with an embroidered border, and trimmed with lace, is distinguishably fashionable'. Their story therefore continues and a few will be shown in this work.

A design of 1803 stated to be 'for a handkerchief or apron' has already been shown in Plate II.7 (p30). This follows the earlier 18th-century convention for a patterned border along the bottom and side edges with additional motifs in the corners but, as in the 18th century, this was by no means the only arrangement current. The apron seen in the fashion illustration in Plate II.44 has solely a decorative border, without corner motifs, while the surviving apron in Plate II.45 has a panel of decoration across the bottom.

The apron in the fashion illustration is surprisingly wide for its date: one might expect it to be narrower to complement the slim line of the dress, like others shown below, but rules on style and decoration of dress in the late 18th to early 19th century were very flexible. The neo-classical design in Plate I.23 (p20) is taken from an apron of similar width (the top, not shown, is altered), as is the example in Plate II.45. The design of this apron is particularly idiosyncratic. Its large willow trees do, however, bear comparison with the large, leafy sprays on the shawl in Plate II.20 (p37) while the spindly stems and tiny leaves of the border sprays are typical of late 18th to early 19th century designs. This combination of factors suggests a date from the 1790s-early 1800s. Decorative, skirt-length aprons like that in Plate II.44 no doubt continued to be worn in later decades of the 19th century but few appear in fashion plates. Those I have seen illustrated from the 1810s onwards are both shorter and narrower: Plate II.46 gives an example from 1812 while a surviving apron shown in Plates II.47, 47a is of similar length and would fall from a high waistline to just below knee level. Unlike the apron in Plate II.46, which is gathered into a waistband, it is cut to taper towards the

Plate II.45 *Drawing of a whiteworked muslin apron with an unusual repeat design of six willow trees above a running design of small trees and upright leafy sprigs worked by tambouring. The design, though unusual, is commensurate with a date in the late 1790s-early 1800s.*
The apron is formed from two fabric widths joined at their selvedges which are whipped together.
Museum of Somerset, Taunton: Cat. No. M 66 Tg.
L - 29½in (75cm); W - 50½in (128cm): waist band - L - 13½in (33.6cm); D - ¾in (2cm); border - D - 1½in to edge (3.8cm); tree - D - 6½in (16.5cm); W - 6in (15cm)

Plate II.45a *A detail showing the tamboured tree and sprig design of the apron in Plate II.45.*

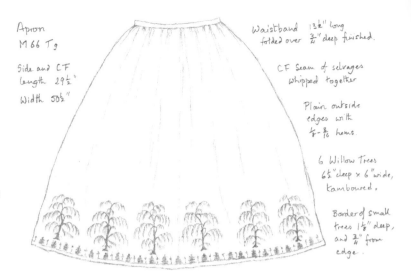

Apron
M 66 Tg

Side and CF
length 29½"
Width 50½"

Waistband 13½" long
folded over ¾" deep finished.

CF Seam of selvages
whipped together

Plain outside
edges with
⅛ - ³⁄₁₆ hems.

6 Willow Trees
6½" deep × 6" wide,
tamboured.

Border of small
trees 1½" deep,
and ¾" from
edge.

Plate II.45b *A closer detail of the apron in Plate II.45.*
The motifs at the bottom are joined by a slightly scalloped line like that forming the actual edge of some items of this period but the bottom edge of this item is a straight hem.

waist in an A-line that matches that of skirts of the mid-late 1810s. Its shaped hemline is not an anomaly as aprons of similar dimensions in other collections also have shaped hemlines (see also Plate II.48).

A further departure from 18th-century norms is the decoration of the waistband but this is only one of several changes in decoration occurring during this period. In the apron in Plate II.47 we see our first use of a tiny pointed edge, a minute form of vandyking. Deep vandyked edges are known from late 18th-early 19th century illustrations of ruffs and collars but are rare in surviving accessories: edges seen in previous illustrations have been straight or finished with small, shallow scallops. It is only in the 1810s that tiny points appear to have gained popularity, with the deeper scallops seen in the apron in Plate II.48 and full vandyking rapidly becoming more popular as well.

The apron in Plates II.48, 48a also shows a novel form of embroidery: it is worked mainly in buttonholed eyelets, foreshadowing the 'broderie anglaise' of later years. Similar embroidery was already in use on larger dress items, such as bodices and skirt flounces, by the late 1810s and further examples are seen in the aprons in Plates II.49 and II.51. That in Plate II.49 also has the unusual feature of being made with a sleeveless bodice rather like that shown in the fashion illustration of 1818 in Plate II.50.

Plate II.46 (top) *Illustration from La Belle Assemblée of 1812. The lady wears a dark red evening robe and a white apron which falls from her high waistline to just below knee level. The waistband appears to be decorated to match her bodice, a new feature of aprons seen repeatedly in the first half of the century. A small kerchief is knotted loosely round the lady's neck.*

Plate II.47a (bottom) *Detail of the apron in Plate II.47. The embroidery is amateur work and comprises rows of minute leaf shapes and overcast eyelets inside an edge of tiny buttonholed points. The three stiff flower sprigs have inserted net fillings: it is impossible to tell whether these are of point ground bobbin net or Heathcoat's machine copy, available from 1809.*

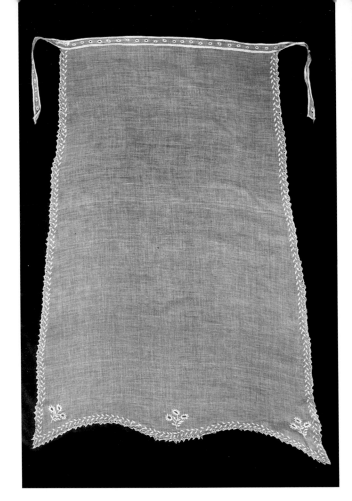

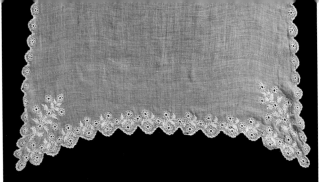

Plate II.48 (above) *Lower part of an apron in the Hereford M &
AG, Cat. No. 3174.*
Only the lower part is shown as the top has been altered.
The tapered shape, similar to that of the apron in Plate II.47, again
suggests a date in the mid-late 1810s though the more complex
decoration suggests it may be marginally later. The running floral
design and scalloped lower edge are very similar to those of the ruff
in Plates II.63-II.63b (p65) but the corner sprays have a stiffness of
character common in the early 19th century.

Plate II.47 (above) *Apron; c1810-20: Hereford M & AG;
Cat. No. 5672.*
The shape of this apron suggests a date in the mid-late 1810s as it
complements the A-line shape of skirts of the period. The simple
decoration extends to the waistband.
CF - 26in (66cm); sides - 31in/33in (79cm/83.5cm); W - at waist -
15in (38cm); W at bottom - 25in (63cm)

Plate II.48a (bottom right) *Detail of the apron in Plate II.48.*
The use of buttonholed eyelets to create a large part of a design was
becoming common on gowns from the late 1810s and is probably the
forerunner of 'broderie anglaise'. Leaves are in padded satin stitch and
stems are trailed, giving a clear contrast with the sheer muslin ground.

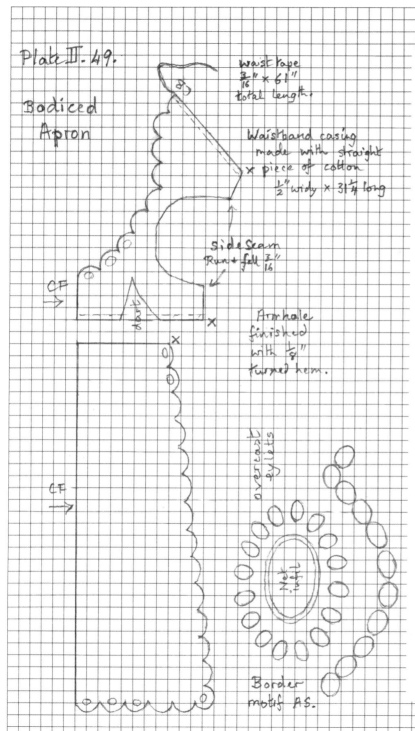

Plate II. 49.

Bodiced
Apron

Waist tape
$\frac{3}{16}'' \times 61''$
total length.

Waistband casing
made with straight
× piece of cotton
$\frac{1}{2}''$ wide × $31\frac{1}{4}$ long

Side seam
Run + fell $\frac{3}{16}''$

Armhole
finished
with $\frac{1}{8}''$
turned hem.

CF

CF

dart

overcast eyelets

Border
motif A.S.

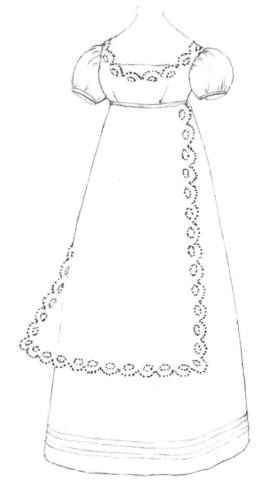

Plate II.49 (above) *Drawing of an apron with a sleeveless bodice, c.1815-20, as in wear: Platt Hall, Manchester; Cat. No. 1947.1213*

The apron's pattern consists entirely of eyelets and larger holes filled with plain net. All the cut edges are neatened with buttonhole stitch. The lightly scalloped edge is formed by a line of touching eyelets.

Plate II.49a (left) *Pattern for the apron in Plate II.49.*

Plate II.50 (left) *Fashion illustration from La Belle Assemblée of January 1818 showing a lady wearing a high-waisted, sleeveless blue robe over a white shirt, or blouse, with a white ruff around her neck. Over the robe is a black apron with a very low-cut sleeveless bodice. The apron appears to be decorated with a ruffle of fabric around its edges.*

Plate II.51 (top right) *Decorative apron in a firm cotton fabric: probably 1810s-1820s; Museum of Somerset, Taunton, Cat. No.397 OSDD467(b). This apron has a similar taper to the aprons in Plates II.47, II.48 suggesting it was worn over a fairly narrow skirt but it is fairly short and its floral sprays are distinctly curved, a common design feature of the 1820s. The very neat scalloping of the edge is unusual at this early date making dating very uncertain. Ls - 25¼in (64cm); CF - 24in (61cm); W max - 22in (56cm)*

Plate II.51a (bottom right) *Detail of the apron in Plate II.51. The decoration, formed largely of overcast eyelets in simple shapes, is another early example of 'broderie anglaise'. The diamond shapes are worked with two lines of backstitch: stems are in satin stitch and trailing. Bold designs like this were popular particularly on skirt flounces in the 1820s.*

Aprons continued: the 1820s to 1830s

The next few aprons are dealt with here as they are somewhat anomalous in the more general whitework story of the 1820s-30s. I have found no contemporary illustrations of whiteworked aprons from the 1820s and 1830s: we are therefore reliant on a few depictions of lace and coloured aprons for an idea of the fashionable styles and proportions of the time. The depiction in Plate II.53 shows that, in the 1830s, decorative aprons still reached to just below the knee as they had in the 1810s but were more gathered into the waist so that they splayed out in line with the fuller skirts of the period. Surviving examples which can be dated to the 1820s-30s by their decoration are similarly gathered.

One apron that, from its size and decoration, probably dates from the 1820s is shown in Plate II.52. In particular it has a wide hem which, because of the semi-transparency of the muslin, forms a dense, contrasting border: similar, but even deeper hems were an extremely common decorative feature of dress from the mid 1820s into the 1830s. The aprons shown in Plates II.54-II.55 may also date from the 1820s but are slightly wider and could therefore be of slightly later date.

Plate II.52 (top) *Decorative apron: probably 1820s, possibly early 1830s.*

This apron, in fine muslin, is slightly gathered into the waistband, suggesting it was worn over a later, fuller skirt than those in Plates II.47 to II.51. The purely linear decoration inside the wide hem is created with an applied braid, a common practice in the 1820s-30s. The waistband is also decorated with the braid.

Various braids were available for this type of work: another example is shown in Plates II.55a and b.

L - 33½in (85cm) + waistband 1¾in (4.5cm)
W max - 33½in (85cm); L waist - 11in (28cm)
Hems - side 2in (5cm), bottom 2¼in (5.7cm)

Plate II.52a (bottom) *Detail of the apron in Plate II.52.*

The next two aprons have one particular feature in common with the apron in the fashion illustration of 1833 (Plate II.53): they both have pockets. In other respects their decoration is very simple. One merely has a scalloped and buttonholed edge and floral motifs in the bottom corners and on the pockets. The other (only details shown) has a sinuous laurel trail worked in applied braid inside a deep hem like that of the apron in Plate II.52. The braid also forms corner motifs and decorates the waistband. An apron (not shown) in the Worthing collection has an almost identical hem and laurel trail but worked in satin stitch. It also has a narrow point-ground bobbin lace trimming but no other decoration.

Plate II.54 (above) Muslin apron; probably late 1820s-mid 1830s. (See p60 for detail)
The embroidery is very simple, probably amateur work, but accords with the general fashions of the 1820s-30s for discrete floral motifs and scalloped edges. The pockets are similar to those illustrated in Plate II.53.
CF - 33¼in (84.5cm); W hem - 41in (104cm); W gathered - 12¼in (31cm); L ties - 33in, 33½in (84cm, 85cm): Pocket: D - 3½in (9cm); W - 4in (10cm).

Plate II.53 (above) Detail from a fashion illustration of 1833 showing a lady wearing a black satin apron over a printed cotton dress. The apron falls to just below knee level and is gathered into an exaggeratedly narrow waist so that its shape follows the line of the typical bell-shaped skirt of the period. The main panel has a line of coloured embroidery inside a wide hem and matching decoration on the waistband. What is new here is a pair of embroidered shield-shaped pockets on the main panel and added wings over the shoulders: these are not universal features of aprons of the period. A portrait (not shown) of Queen Victoria depicts her wearing a very similar apron in 1837-8.

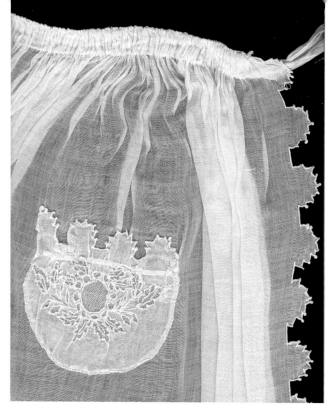

Plate II.54a (left) Detail of the apron in Plate II.54 showing the gathering of the fabric into the waistband and one of the two pockets. The pockets have scalloped upper edges matching the complex scalloping of the apron edge. The fillings in the large holes are of embroidered net.

Plate II.55a (below left) Detail of a muslin apron; probably late 1820s-mid 1830s: Worthing M & AG. Cat. No. 1971/1132 The main embroidery is in applied braid with a pulled-thread filling in the corner motif and overcast eyelets for additional decoration. A similar applied braid is shown in more detail in Plate II.80b.

Plate II.55b (below right) A pocket of the apron in Plate II.55a.

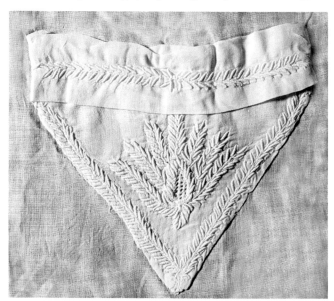

THE 1820s
Kerchiefs, or fichus, and square shawls

The aprons just seen fit into the overall decorative schemes
of the 1820s-30s but are not illustrative of their more
common features which will be seen in the following pages.
At the beginning of the 1820s, designs still consisted largely
of narrow borders as they had in the 1800s-1810s and motifs
were still small and relatively simple, worked mainly in tiny
areas of padded satin stitch with trailed lines. Floral sprays
with C-shaped curvature were, however, already in evidence,
replacing the earlier stiffer sprigs. Throughout the 1820s they
were to remain largely separate, or discrete, and repetitive but
they dominated the design scene: neo-classicism was
definitely passé.

The new designs were widely distributed in published
patterns, a few of which are illustrated in Plates II.56, II.57.
There are also many surviving compilations of patterns,
drawn by both amateurs and professionals, which clearly date
from the 1820s and 1830s but, unfortunately, few are
inscribed with names or dates. According to their captions,
many were suitable for either lace or muslin embroidery.
These designs were available for use on all the white
accessories of the period which proliferated as coloured
dresses returned to favour. Before continuing the story of
more important items, however, we shall finish the story of
whiteworked kerchiefs.

1820s GEORGE IV ON THE THRONE; SIR ROBERT PEEL
CREATES THE LONDON POLICE FORCE;
EARLY ELASTICATED GOODS

1821 STEAM PASSENGER SERVICE DOVER/CALAIS

1822 GEORGE IV VISITS SCOTLAND;
CHARLES MACINTOSH MAKES FIRST RUBBERISED
WATERPROOF FABRIC

1824 DEATH OF BYRON AT MISSOLONGHI:
BEETHOVEN'S 9TH SYMPHONY

1824-5 TRADE UNIONS LEGALISED

1825 INAUGURAL RUN OF THE ROCKET DRAWING THE
FIRST PASSENGER-CARRYING STEAM TRAIN

1828 HEILMANN'S PATENT FOR THE 'HANDMACHINE'
WHICH PRODUCED A GOOD IMITATION OF HAND EMBROIDERY

Plate II.56, II.57 Muslin embroidery patterns for 1823 from the
magazine 'Ackermann's Repository'. The repeated curving sprigs are
typical of border designs of the 1820s. All might have been worked
along a lightly scalloped edge like that shown in the bottom
example. All are composed of slender stems and tiny leaf or petal
shapes, some of which are shaded in and were no doubt intended to
be worked in padded satin stitch while others are open and could be
worked as eyelets. The top example also has spaces for filling stitches
while the bottom one shows that grounds might still be powdered
with sprigs.

By the 1820s, the white kerchief as it had been known and worn from the 18th century was dying out, though not dead: habit shirts could provide the necessary warmth and modesty with low necklines in the daytime and the decorated puffed sleeves that had become the mode by 1820 were not to be hidden by enveloping muslin. There was also less use of kerchiefs and similar articles over the carefully dressed hair. The examples shown in Plates II.58 to II.60 are exceptions.

The half-kerchief worn over the hair in Plate II.58, dated 1822, is described as a 'fichu of fine blond', i.e. of blonde silk bobbin lace: here we have the relatively new use in English of the French word 'fichu' for a triangular accessory. The lady also wears a voluminous 'cachemire shawl' but it is stated that both the fichu and the shawl would only be worn for leaving the theatre or party: the lady's elaborate hairstyle and her bodice and sleeves, trimmed to match the elaborate decoration of her skirt, would be revealed indoors.

Plate II.59 shows a whiteworked kerchief or fichu which could well have been worn over the head in the manner shown in Plate II.58. Its repetitive border of floral sprays within a scalloped edge looks very similar to that of the fichu in the fashion plate and also resembles the embroidery patterns of 1823 in Plate II.56, 57. It could alternatively have been draped round the shoulders like that in Plate II.60 but this latter, like the fichu in Plate II.58, is stated to be of lace so it would not hide the shoulder line completely. It is described as a 'pointe', the French term for

Plate II.58 Fashion illustration from La Belle Assemblée for 1822 showing Parisian evening dress.

The lady wears a roughly triangular kerchief described as a 'fichu of fine blond' folded and worn over her head. Its edge is bordered by discrete flower sprays that curve into the scalloped edge: the centre is also patterned.

The lady also wears a large rectangular 'cachemire' shawl of the same basic design as that shown in Plates II.25-II.28: only its width is different but shawls of similar width were also worn earlier. Both kerchief and shawl were intended to be removed indoors.

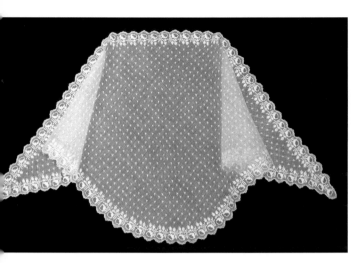

Chapeau de sparterie, garni en gaze. Robe de mousseline imprimée, à corsage de velours simulé. Pointe de dentelle.

Plate II.59 (above) *Muslin kerchief or fichu: probably early 1820s. This might have been worn over the head or round the shoulders but is unlikely to have been tucked into the bodice as was common in the 18th century. The discrete rose sprigs in the border are slightly stiff but similar in scale, complexity and closeness to sprays in Plate II.56. See p64 for detail*

a triangular shawl: the illustration shows a complete square folded on the diagonal to form a triangle.

A rather larger whiteworked square which may have been worn in a manner similar to that in Plate II.60 is shown in Plates II.61, 61a. By the 1820s, this would almost certainly have been called a shawl rather than a kerchief or buffon. It is perhaps mainly the mode of wear that distinguishes this 19th-century shawl from a late 18th century kerchief: rather than simply covering and filling the neckline and perhaps shoulders, it would have enveloped the torso.

Looking again at Plate II.60, it is seen that, in addition to the shawl, the lady wears a double collar which falls from high around her neck just onto her shoulders. It is the development of such collars and other neckwear that we shall explore next.

Plate II.60 (above) *Fashion illustration of 1823.*
The lady wears a printed blue muslin dress with a square of fabric folded into a triangle round her shoulders. It is stated to be of 'lace', not whitework, but its pattern of discrete floral motifs within a scalloped edge would be equally appropriate in whitework.

Plate II.59a (above) Detail of the kerchief in Plate II.59.
The embroidery is worked in lightly padded satin stitch and trailing with pulled-thread fillings; the 'spot' design in the centre was very common in the 1800s-1820s; the lightly scalloped edge is buttonholed outside a row of overcast eyelets.

Plate II.61a (above) Detail of the shawl in Plate II.61.
The motifs, though fairly large, are composed of small areas of padded satin stitch and overcast eyelets. The lightly-scalloped buttonholed edge borders a band of openwork between trailed lines.

Plate II.61 (left) Square shawl: probably mid-late 1820s.
This fine muslin square would have been worn round the shoulders like the accessories shown in Plates II.58 and II.60. It is larger than most earlier kerchiefs to accommodate the fuller sleeve heads of the later 1820s and would probably have been called a shawl. Its nearly symmetrical border motifs bear a strong resemblance to those of a pattern in Ackermann's Repository of 1828 (Plate II.62).

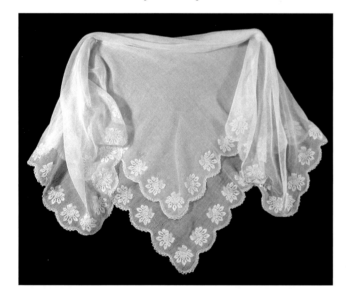

Plate II.62 (right) Pattern for muslin embroidery from Ackermann's Repository of 1828. The right-hand motif, with its C-shaped curvature, is very characteristic of the period. The symmetry of the left-hand motif was much less common in the 1820s.

Ruffs, collars, pelerines and canezous

Several fashion plates shown in previous pages have depicted ladies wearing ruffs and a further example is given in Plate II.64 (p66). These took their inspiration from late 16th and early 17th century collars depicted particularly by van Dyck and these in turn derived their designs and pointed edges from Mediaeval Gothic styles. From the late 18th century these had been part of the trend for wearing romanticised versions of past fashions: they appeared anachronistically with the neo-classical dress of the 1790s–1810s but continued into the 1830s as the Gothic style came to influence dress as a whole.

If the dictates of fashion magazines were obeyed, most ruffs were of lace rather than whitework but few original examples in either medium survive: Plates II.63–II.63.b show one of the few in whitework. This has three frills gathered and whipped to a neckband. Each frill has a buttonholed scalloped edge with a row of overcast eyelets inside it bordering a sinuous flowing stem with alternate flower heads and leafy sprays springing from opposite sides. The border is thus very similar in character to that of the lower edge of the apron in Plate II.48, although on a rather smaller scale.

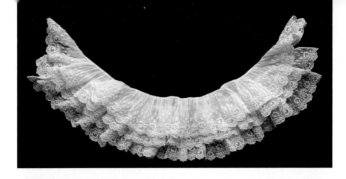

Plate II.63 Triple ruff shown with its three layers superimposed as in wear: late 1810s-1820s.
Neck band L - 16¼in (47.6cm); D - 2in (5cm)
Frills - D - 2½in (6.5cm); L - 41¼in (105cm)

Plate II.63a The triple ruff of Plate II.63 showing the attachment of the layers to the neckband, one in the centre and two at the edges.

Plate II.63b Detail of the triple ruff of Plate II.63.
The embroidery is in padded satin stitch, trailing and overcast eyelets with a buttonholed edge. The fillings are of pulled-thread work. The scale and curving form of the embroidered sprays are similar to those of the discrete sprays in Plate II.56 suggesting a date for this ruff in the early 1820s but a date of any time between the early 1810s and early 1830s is possible.

Plate II.64 (above) *Engraving c.1820 entitled 'The Miniature '*
The lady (left), holding the miniature, wears a ruff with two or three layers: this may be attached to, or separate from, the chemisette which fills her low neckline and has embroidered insertions on the shoulders. The lady in the centre wears a standing collar which opens in a V-shape down the front and consists of at least two layers with scalloped edges: it is probably sewn to the white gown worn beneath the outer garment which has patterned bands down its front opening.

Plate II.65 (right) *Detail from a fashion illustration in La Belle Assemblée of 1814 (Harris M & AG).*
The lady's deeply vandyked collar is stiffened to stand out from her neck. It is made from a different fabric from the coloured dress material. It might have been tacked into place quickly for wear, being removable equally quickly for washing.

The illustration in Plate II.64, in addition to the lady with the ruff already mentioned, includes a lady wearing a collar with a V-neckline. This, like the standing bands and turn-down collars seen previously, is probably part of a white garment, in this case a dress, in other cases a habit shirt or chemisette. While white was fashionable, whiteworked collars could be incorporated in the robes of the period and are not usually identifiable as separate accessories except in the form of ruffs. Once coloured fabrics started to become fashionable again in the later 1810s, white neckwear regained its earlier importance in providing an attractive, washable barrier between wearer and more expensive dress fabrics that were difficult to clean. White collars might then be made as separate accessories with a neckband for sewing into the neckline of a gown but could still be incorporated in larger accessories such as chemisettes.

As few collars survive from this early period, we are reliant on a few, comparatively rare, contemporary illustrations for evidence of their development. An example of a white collar that was clearly made separately as it is worn with a high-necked, coloured gown is shown in Plate II.65. Such a collar would presumably have been starched to make it stand out from the neck as shown but two further illustrations of the same year, 1814, (Plates II.66 and II.67) show turn-down collars: these would probably have been made up with the gowns but show the general styles of the period.

As collars grew during the 1820s, their rôle changed. They were usually designed to fall from a high neckline, particularly at the back and, as they came to cover more of the shoulders, they could provide some of the warmth previously provided by kerchiefs. The larger ones also came to be known by a new name, the 'pelerine'. These were often independent accessories, finished at the neck by a narrow hem or seamed along the neckline to one or more additional layers of fabric to form double or triple pelerines. Being designed simply to sit around the neck, they might be held in place by pins or a brooch, or they might, like collars, be attached to a chemisette or even a dress, the distinction between the two accessories being merely one of size and certainly not exact.

Two examples which probably date from the first half of the 1820s are illustrated in Plates II.71 and II.72 but dating is not definitive as, although later examples became larger and more elaborate, simpler ones continued to be worn through into the 1830s. These two examples both show a form of edge decoration which became very common in the 1820s-30s: the edge is not only cut into large points or scallops but is also finished with minute points or scallops, the whole being buttonholed.

Plate II.66 (right bottom) Detail from an illustration showing 'Fashionable and elegant dresses for the year 1814' (from a scrap album, Hereford M & AG).
The lady's white robe has a turn-down collar with a vandyked edge probably made up with the dress. This form of collar, with front edges flaring away from each other, was termed a 'square collar', distinguishing it from a 'round collar' seen in Plate II.67.

Plate II.67 (above) Detail from a fashion illustration from the early 1810s showing a lady in morning dress wearing a 'round' collar, the front edges of which meet. The collar appears to be embroidered to match the vandyked border of her outer garment, a pelisse. She also wears a plain, pale yellow kerchief over a decorated cap on her head. (Harris M & AG)

Plate II.68 (above) *Detail from a fashion illustration of 1823. The lady wears 'Marine dress' comprising a 'pelisse of marshmallow blossom coloured Gros de Naples' with a 'white colarette of fine muslin… trimmed with Mechlin lace'. Similar collars can still be seen in fashion plates of the 1830s while the contemporary portrait in Plate II.69 shows a much wider double pelerine.*

Plate II.70 (left) *Detail from a fashion illustration of 1825: Harris M & AG.*
The lady wears 'carriage dress' with a whiteworked collar over a pelerine of the dress material.

Plate II.69 (above) *Detail from a portrait of Mrs. Holland, an author, from La Belle Assemblée for 1823.*
Mrs. Holland wears a combination of newer and older fashions: a white kerchief tucked into her neckline and a double pelerine, the lower layer of which spreads to the very tips of her shoulders. The two layers are probably trimmed with lace rather than embroidery.

Plate II.71a (opposite bottom left) *Detail of the pelerine in Plate II.71. The sprays bear a strong affinity with those in the patterns of 1823 in Plate II.56. They are worked in tiny areas of padded satin stitch, overcast eyelets and trailing, typical of the first quarter of the century. The tiny points on the slightly scalloped edge are very neatly buttonholed.*

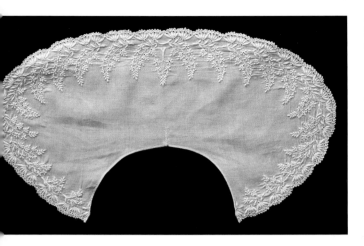

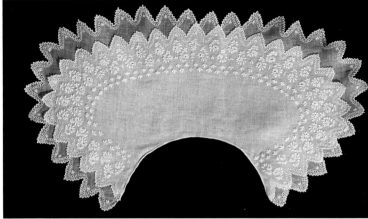

Plate II.71 (above) *Pelerine: early-mid 1820s.*
I include this as a 'pelerine' as its neck edge is not finished with a band that could be sewn into the neckline of a garment. It is of very modest size and may be for a child. The floral sprays are beautifully graduated from smaller ones near the neck edge to the larger, symmetrical one at the centre back. See p75 for pattern

Plate II.72 (above) *Double pelerine: early-mid 1820s.*
This is of similar shape to the pelerine in Plate II.71 but rather larger: its embroidery is equally simple. The lower layer is embroidered only around the edge where the decoration will show in wear. The edges are vandyked, finished with tiny points and buttonholed.
Top layer CB - 7in (18cm); Wmax - 19in (48.2cm)
Bottom layer CB - 8in (20.3cm); Wmax - 21¼in (54cm)
L neck edge - 13in (29.5cm)

Plate II.72a (below) *Detail of the double pelerine in Plate II.72 showing part of the upper layer and the seam joining the two layers on the right.*

The following plates show various forms of collars, pelerines and ruffs from the later 1820s, some perhaps just into the 1830s, many of them as separate accessories, some attached to chemisettes. During this period it was the shape and decoration of that part of the chemisette intended to be seen that was important, not the form and construction of its body. A new accessory, the canezou, will also be introduced.

Plate II.73 (above) Detail from a fashion illustration of 1826 showing a lady in 'Walking Dress' wearing a white double pelerine which falls onto her shoulders. The sleeves are now fuller than in earlier illustrations, the fullness extending down the arms to tight cuffs at the wrists. The very deep hem and vandyked decoration on the skirt were common from the mid 1820s-mid 1830s.

Plate II.74 (above) Double pelerine with vandyked edges; c.1820s (only half shown). Plate I.3 shows a close detail.
The individual curved floral sprays in each point of the vandyking are more complex than in previous examples. The padded satin stitch still occupies small areas but includes some veins and indented edges: fillings in the flower centres are needlepoint stitches.
That the design and embroidery are more complex than seen previously is due to their higher quality rather than a later date: the work is characteristic of Ayrshire embroidery from the 1820s into the mid 19th century. The pelerine would have looked very similar in wear to the pelerine in Plate II.73.
Top layer CB - 4½in (11.5cm); Dmax - 6in (15.2cm);
Bottom layer CB - 8in into point (20.3cm)
See p73 for pattern

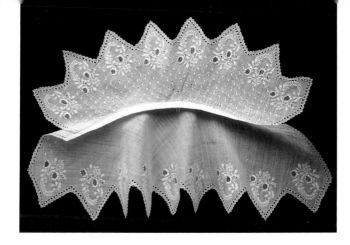

Plate II.74a (above) The double pelerine of Plate II.74 showing the two layers spread apart. The main panel of the upper layer is filled with spot motifs but these are not repeated on the lower layer where they will not be seen.

Plate II.75 (right) Detail from a fashion illustration from The Ladies' Pocket Book of 1829: Walker M & AG.
The lady wears a white vandyked collar, or ruff. She carries a pocket handkerchief in her hand: many fashion plates show ladies carrying some accessory, such as gloves, parasols and bags: pocket handkerchiefs start to appear regularly from about the mid 1820s.

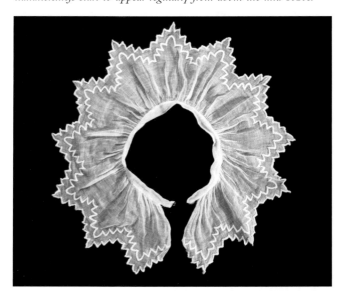

Plate II.76 (left) Whiteworked collar in the form of a ruff: 1820s-early 1830s. The collar is very similar to the one shown in Plate II.75 but similar ruffs can be seen in fashion plates from the 1810s into the 1830s so it cannot be dated exactly. It is formed from a length of muslin gathered and sewn to a neckband along one edge. The free, vandyked edge is buttonholed, as is the decorative line inside the edge. Neck band - L - 15¾in (44cm); D - ½in (1.2cm); ruff - D max - 4¼in (12cm); D min - 3in (7.5cm)

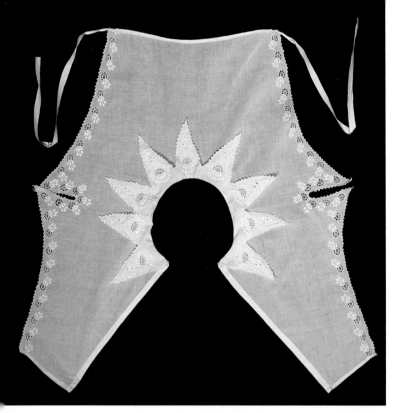

Looking now at Plates II.77-II.77a, a new accessory, the canezou, is shown which is very similar in construction to a chemisette of the period (see Plates II.79, 79a) but is intended to be worn over a bodice rather than under it. The main distinction lies in its decoration which, extending down the outer edges of the front and back panels, is clearly intended to be seen. The hemmed lower edges would be hidden under the wide belt commonly worn in the late 1820s-mid 1830s.

Canezous, like chemisettes, could carry falling collars or pelerines and be front- or back-opening. This example has a high, round neckline and a deeply vandyked collar like the collar of 1814 shown in Plate II.65 but both the shaping of the canezou body and the embroidery style suggest a later date. A more elaborate example is shown in Plate II.105. The term 'canezou' was later applied to a different accessory.

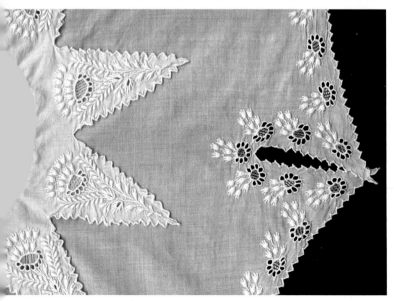

Plate II.77 (top left) *Canezou: probably mid-late 1820s.*
The body of the canezou is cut from a single panel of firm cotton fabric. The decoration down to the waistline suggests that it was worn over rather than under a dress, with the plain waist hems concealed by a belt. The shoulders are decorated with slits forming points which would open in wear to form wings over wide sleeve heads like minor versions of those of the bodice in Plate II.79 or of the canezou in Plate II.105.

Plate II.77a (bottom left) *Detail of the canezou in Plate II.77. The embroidery has a lightness of character similar to that of the pelerine in Plate II.74 but the fillings are of embroidered net rather than needlepoint.*
Body - CB - 12in (30.5cm); CF - 9in (23cm): shoulder width at wings - 8¾in (22cm)

Plate II.78 (right) *Patterns for the canezou in Plates II.77, 77a and the double pelerine in Plate II.74, 74a.*

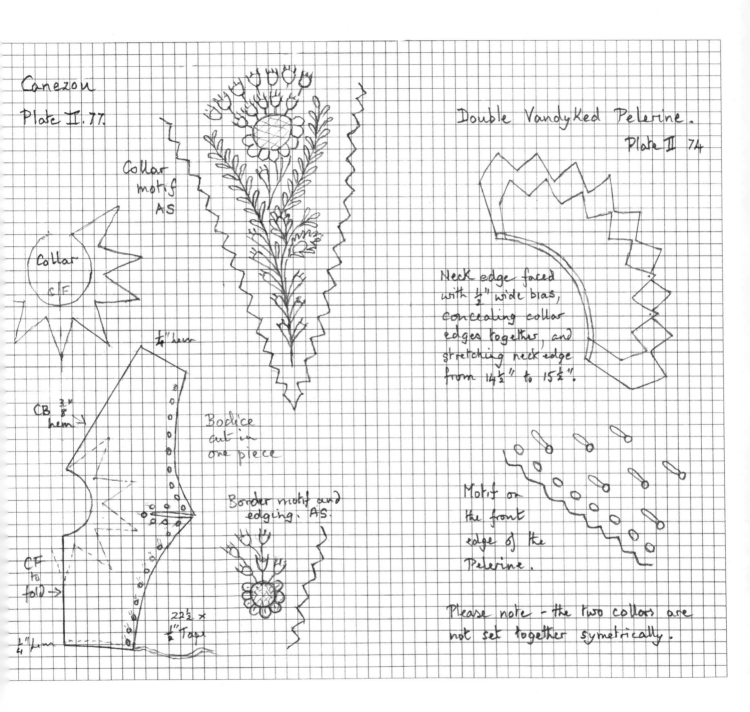

Canezou
Plate II. 77.

Collar motif AS

Collar
C F

Double Vandyked Pelerine.
Plate II 74

¼" hem

Bodice
cut in
one piece

Neck edge faced
with ½" wide bias,
concealing collar
edges together, and
stretching neck edge
from 14½" to 15½".

CB ⅜" hem →

Border motif and
edging. AS.

Motif on
the front
edge of the
Pelerine.

CF
to
fold →

22½ x
1" Tart

¼" hem

Please note - the two collars are
not set together symetrically.

73

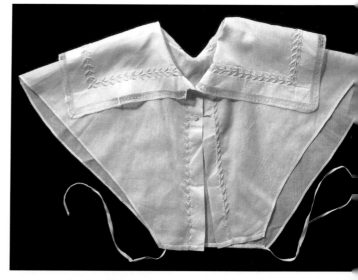

Plate II.79 (above) *Detail from a fashion illustration from La Belle Assemblée of 1827.*

The lady's collar is of a different shape from those seen previously: its square front panels may be part of a single panel which extends round the back of the neck, like those shown previously, or could be separate panels as seen in Plate II.80a.

The lady's bodice is pleated in a V-shape into the waist and finished on the shoulders with divided wings, a common dress feature in the late 1820s-early 1830s.

Plate II.80 (top right) *A front-opening chemisette: mid-late 1820s. The square panels of the collar look very like those of the collar in Plate II.79, even to the lines of decoration parallel to their edges. The front and back panels of the chemisette taper into the waist, a common but by no means universal feature of the period. Their front edges are decorated so the chemisette might be worn under an open neckline. For fastening, two buttons and buttonholes are provided near the neckline with a waist tie at the back.*

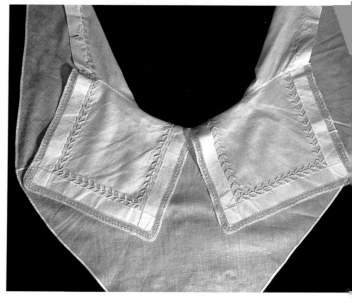

Plate II.80a (above) *Detail of the chemisette in Plate II.80 laid flat to show that the collar comprises simply two rectangular panels of fabric.*

Plate II.80b (right) Detail of the collar in Plate II.80. Each collar panel is decorated with a deep hem like that of the apron in Plate II.52. A simple design in an applied braid runs inside the hem and the edge is trimmed with a narrow Buckinghamshire point bobbin lace. The simple embroidery design is more in keeping with styles of the 1810s than the 1820s but the collar style and depth of the chemisette body determine the date. The decorative braid is more complex than that used on the apron in Plate II.52 but similar to that in Plates II.55a, 55b. It comprises a series of fat portions connected by tapered ends imitating the tiny padded-satin-stitch leaf shapes common in embroidery of the 1810s-20s. It is couched down in a continuous process: a first fat portion forms a section of stem; two portions are taken to one side to form a leaf; the next two portions form a leaf on the other side; the stem is then continued, and so on. At first glance, the result looks like whitework embroidery in trailing and padded satin stitch but is much quicker to work.

Plate II.81 (below) Patterns for the chemisette in Plates II.80-80b and the pelerine in Plate II.71.

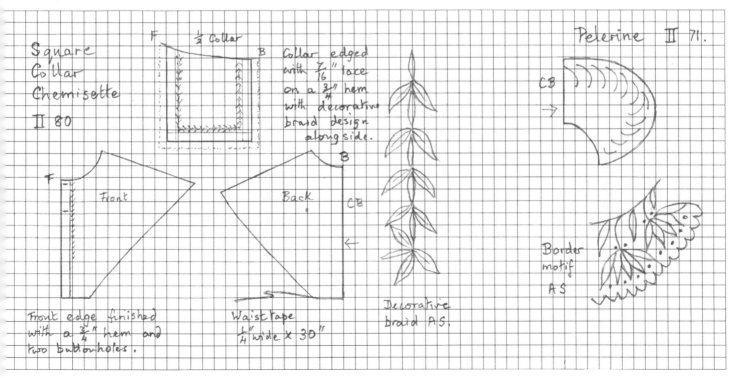

75

The almost square corners and deep hem of the next pelerine (Plate II.82) make it look remarkably similar, when worn, to the collar of the chemisette in Plate II.80. The main difference lies in the inclusion of large curved floral sprays in the corners: a detail of one corner is shown in Plate I.29, p21. The sprays are larger and more complex than the corner motifs seen in kerchiefs and aprons in the 1800s–1810s but are compact and isolated. Their development in the 1820s was most probably influenced by the boteh of Kashmiri designs: they became common features in lace and other textiles well into the 1830s so it is not surprising to see them used in whitework as well. Patterns in Plate II.83, 84 give two examples dated 1825 while the portrait in Plate II.86 shows a collar or pelerine in wear.

In yet another surviving pelerine shown in Plate II.87 the deep hems and embroidered borders of the items described above are replaced by a whiteworked band of similar width inside a tiny dentate edge. Many other patterns from this period survive and three more are illustrated in Plates II.85, II.88 and II.89.

Plate II.82 (below) Whiteworked pelerine, mid-late 1820s. The inner edge of the deep hem is neatened with a narrow band of openwork between trailed lines. Inside that is a very simple embroidered border with a very large floral spray in each corner. The embroidery is worked in very narrow areas of padded satin stitch with clefts in many features of the main sprays.
L (outer edge) - 30in (76cm); L (neck edge) - 19in (48cm); CB - 7in (17.7cm); Hem D - 1½in (1.7cm); front edge - 10in (25.3cm)

Plate II.83 (opposite top left), II.84 (opposite left middle) Two embroidery patterns from an album of hand-drawn patterns showing designs for large, curving sprays and scalloped borders. One spray has distinct C-shaped curvature while the other is simply asymmetric. The pages are inscribed 'Miss Smith xxx July 1825' and 'Miss Smith June 1825 xxx'.

Plate II.85 (opposite bottom left) Embroidery pattern for the corner of a collar or pelerine: this was published by the firm G & R Turner which went out of business in 1830: it probably dates from the late 1820s.

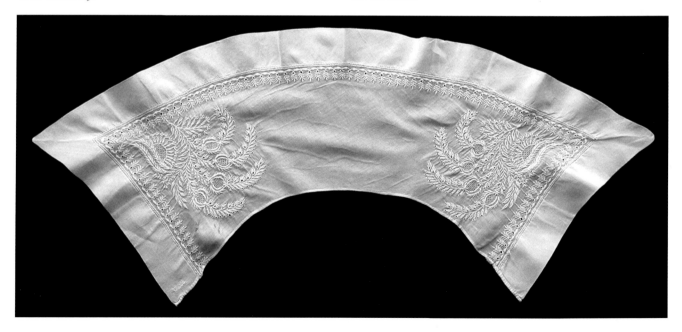

Plate II.86 (above) Portrait of Mrs. Anne Carlisle: late 1820s.
© *Leeds Museums and Galleries (Abbey House). Mrs. Carlisle wears a whiteworked collar or pelerine with a deep hem of similar width to that of the pelerine in Plate II.82 but with a deeply vandyked edge: a large curving floral spray decorates each of the front corners. Her bonnet may be finished with a lace or whitework frill: the repeated, curved floral motifs in the points would have been fashionable in either medium.*

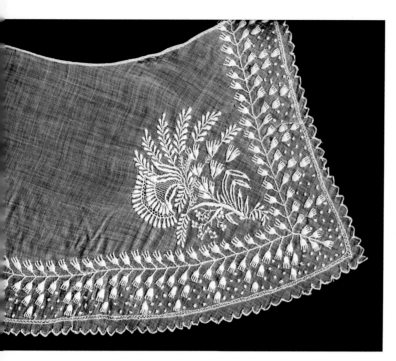

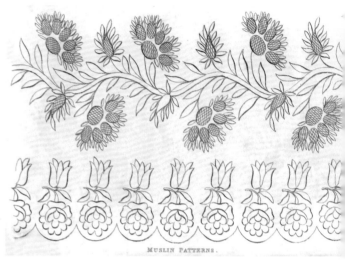

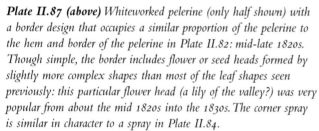

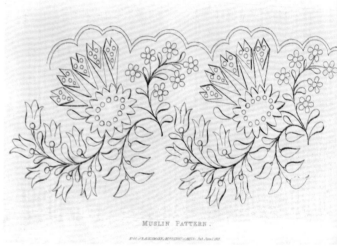

Plate II.87 (above) *Whiteworked pelerine (only half shown) with a border design that occupies a similar proportion of the pelerine to the hem and border of the pelerine in Plate II.82: mid-late 1820s. Though simple, the border includes flower or seed heads formed by slightly more complex shapes than most of the leaf shapes seen previously: this particular flower head (a lily of the valley?) was very popular from about the mid 1820s into the 1830s. The corner spray is similar in character to a spray in Plate II.84.*
The outer edge is slightly curved and finished with tiny buttonholed scallops.
L outer edge - 27½in (70cm); L neck edge - 17½in (44.5cm); CB - 7½in (19th cm); D border - 2in (5cm); front edge - 7¾in (19.7cm)

Plate II.88 (top right) *Muslin embroidery pattern from Ackermann's Repository of 1828 showing a very simple, repetitive border and a continuous trailing design.*

Plate II.89 (above) *Muslin embroidery pattern for a border from Ackermann's Repository of 1828, the same year as the design above. This border is more complex than those in Plates II.83-85 and II.87: it is formed by discrete motifs that are not joined to a continuously flowing stem but touch to form a continuous band of decoration.*

THE LATE 1820s TO 1830s
Pelerines, fichu pelerines and canezous

In previous pages we have seen how dress from the 1790s through into the 1810s was inspired by romantic ideas of the past, whether the flowing garments of classical antiquity or the gothic revival in vandyked edges. By the 1820s the neoclassical influence had died but vandyked edges did not simply remain but proliferated. By the end of the decade, historical revivalism had moved on to the period of Charles I. Skirts and sleeves that had been expanding slowly put on a rapid spurt. The new silhouette was that of a cavalier's lady, even to the wide-brimmed hats and spectacular falling collars of the 1630s–40s.

Plate II.91 (above) Double pelerine: probably mid-late 1820s. This would have been worn like the pelerine in Plate II.90. Both layers of the pelerine have vandyked edges which are further cut into tiny points: a floral motif with distinct C-shaped curvature occupies each large point. See Plate I.27, p21 for a detail.
L neck edge - 16in (41cm); D pattern - 1⅜in (3.4cm)
Top layer - CB - 9in (23cm); Wmax - 21¼in (54cm) Bottom layer - CB into point - 11¼in (28.5cm); Wmax - 23in (58.5cm)

Plate II.90 (right) Fashion illustration from the 'Ladies' Pocket Magazine' for November 1830 showing morning dress. The lady's very full sleeves, bell-shaped skirt with its deep band of decoration round the bottom and the extravagant confection on her head are typical of fashion in the late 1820s-very early 1830s. With the outfit she wears a wide white collar or pelerine with a vandyked edge which extends just to the points of her shoulders: a discrete floral motif extends into each point. The collar is worn high round the back of the neck: this is typical of collars through from the early 1800s into the later 1830s, whether they are high and closed at the front or open in a V shape.

These new fashions were realised in exuberant pelerines that spread to cover the higher, wider shoulder line. The extravagant use of fabric was matched by their decoration. Edges became more deeply vandyked or scalloped. Simple curved sprigs grew into more complex, more densely patterned versions. Larger areas of padded satin stitch developed indented edges and grooved centres that could depict larger leaf and flower shapes.

As time went on the designs spread away from the borders and might cover the entire ground, becoming more rococo in style, more curvaceous and flowing. A greater variety of stitches was introduced, particularly with greater use of fillings, whether of needlepoint, pulled-thread work or embroidered net. The next few plates will show some modest examples of this development with the more fantastical results to follow.

Plate II.92 (above left) Double pelerine, mid 1820s-early 1830s, shown from the back as in wear. (Hereford M & AG)
This is very similar in shape and size to the pelerine in Plate II.91. The decoration is also similar in character but slightly fuller and more complex: it may be the later of the two but they could well be contemporary - the wide variation in designs of the period is demonstrated by the patterns on pages 77, 78.
Top layer - L neck edge - 14in (35.5cm); CB - 7½in (19cm); Wmax - 19½in (49.5cm)
Bottom layer - CB - 9½in (24cm); Wmax - 23in (58.5cm)

Plate II.92a (left) Detail of the pelerine in Plate II.92.
The points of each layer are occupied by symmetrical motifs with discrete curving sprays above them which spread further into the ground than those on the pelerine in Plate II.91. The compact triangular sprays in the lower layer are beautifully arranged to accommodate the points of the upper layer.
The padded satin stitch is divided by veins and indented edges but the motifs are still very bold.

Plate II.93 (above) *Double pelerine: probably early 1830s;*
St. Fagans Cat. No. 59.176-36
This pelerine is not as deep as those in Plates II.91 and II.92.
The border sprigs are very simple but complemented by much larger
floral designs spreading from the corners of the upper layer. The
embroidery is still bold, worked in small areas of padded satin
stitch, some with indented edges, suggesting that this is of
comparable date to the pelerines in Plates II.91 and II.92 but the
spreading design suggests that this may be the latest of the group.

Plate II.94 (right) *Detail from a single pelerine carried by a*
chemisette; late 1820s-early 1830s; Devonshire Collection. This is
aesthetically similar to the pelerine in Plate II.93 but the corner
motif is a simple curved spray. Such motifs continued in use into the
mid 1830s alongside the spreading form seen in Plate II.93.
The motifs are worked almost entirely in tiny areas of padded satin
stitch and trailing with pulled fillings.

Plate II.96 (above) *Double pelerine, probably late 1820s-early 1830s.*
This pelerine is wide and shallow and may have looked like the pelerine in Plate II.95 when worn. The upper layer is beautifully cut into concave scallops to accommodate the sprigs in the convexly-curved scallops of the lower layer. Both layers are cut on the cross. The bold design is created by a combination of large overcast eyelets and tiny areas of lightly-padded satin stitch with trailed stems.

Plate II.95 (above) *Detail from a fashion illustration from the 'Lady's Magazine' of 1829 showing walking dress.*
The lady wears a typical wide-brimmed hat of the late 1820s, full sleeves, a whiteworked pelerine and a ruff. The pelerine fits more closely round the neck and is cut straighter from the neckline onto the shoulders than that in Plate II.90, showing the variation in pelerine styles of the period.

Plate II.96a (bottom right) *Detail of the pelerine in Plate II.96. The large filling is embroidered net. See p83 for pattern*

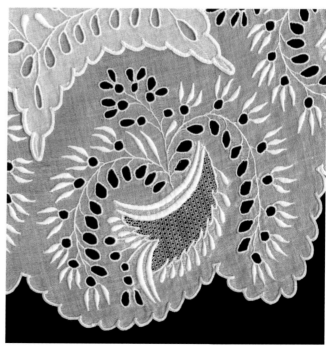

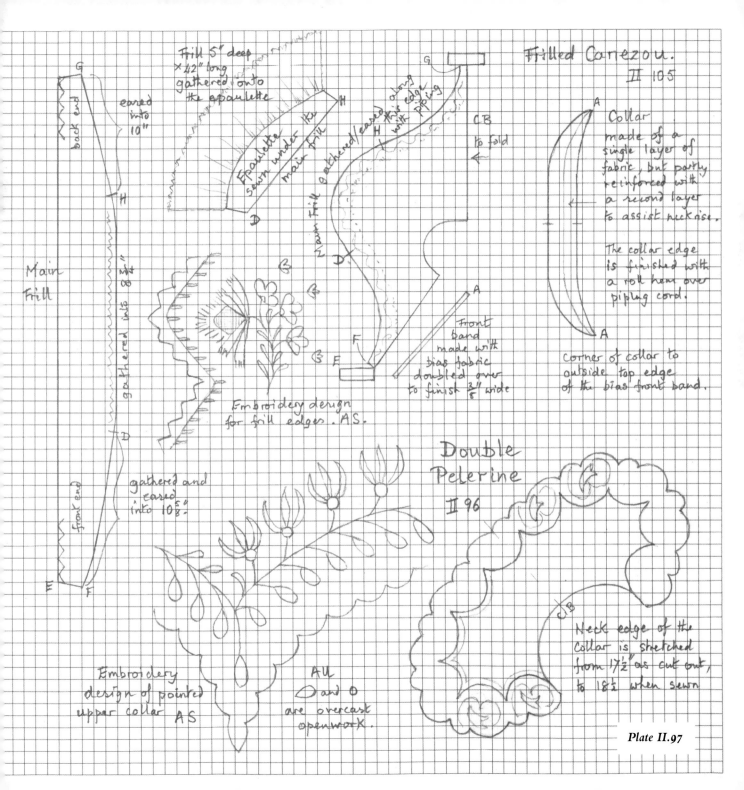

Frill 5" deep × 42" long gathered onto the epaulette

Frilled Carezou.
II 105

eared into 10"

back end

Epaulette sewn under main frill

Main frill gathered/eared along this edge with pipping

G

H

CB
to fold

Main Frill

gathered into 8"

Collar made of a single layer of fabric, but partly reinforced with a second layer to assist neck rise.

The collar edge is finished with a roll hem over piping cord.

A

A

Front band made with bias fabric doubled over to finish 3/8" wide

Corner of collar to outside top edge of the bias front band.

Embroidery design for frill edges. AS.

front end

gathered and eared into 10 5/8".

E

F

Double Pelerine
II 96

Neck edge of the Collar is stretched from 17½" as cut out, to 18½" when sewn

Embroidery design of pointed upper collar AS

All ⊘ and ⊘ are overcast openwork.

Plate II.97

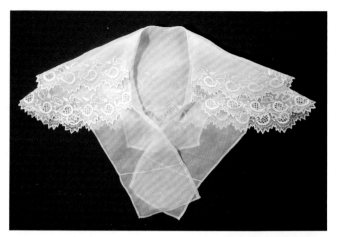

Plate II.98 *Detail from a fashion illustration of the very early 1830s: Harris M & AG*

The lady wears a canezou with a cross-over bodice and a triple pelerine which may be a separate accessory. The front edges of the pelerine are set very wide apart at the neckline. The pelerine in Plate II.99 does not sit happily round the neck with the front panels of the chemisette meeting in the normal manner: perhaps they should be crossed, as shown, or perhaps the fact that there is no sign of wear means that the chemisette was never worn.

Plate II.100 (above) *Double pelerine in a firm cotton fabric: mid 1820s-early 1830s: Worcester collection, Cat. No. 66/1229*
This example has a higher, rounder neck and is deeper at the front than other pelerines shown: although this form is less common, it is by no means unique in collections. The use of concave and convex curves to edge the two layers has already been seen in Plate II.96. The design includes four large curved flower sprays and a central symmetrical spray on the upper layer and elongate sprays round the edge of the lower layer. Top layer: CF - 6in (15cm); CB - 7¾in (19.6cm), Lower layer: CF - 7in (17.8cm); CB - 9½in (24cm)

Plate II.99 (opposite top right) *Chemisette with a double pelerine in pina cloth; probably Philippine work, early 1830s. The two pelerines of this accessory are again similar in shape to those in Plates II.93, 94 and their embroidery occupies a similar position: they may have looked rather like the pelerines of the accessory in Plate II.98 in wear but with the chemisette tucked inside the bodice. It is made in pina cloth, the fine, semi-transparent, creamy-coloured material made in the Far East from fibres from a member of the pineapple family.*

Plate II.99a (opposite bottom right) *Detail of one of the pelerines in Plate II.99: the embroidery designs on the two pelerines are identical. The embroidery style is rather different from the European norm for the early 1830s: the shapes of the motifs; the use of satin stitch rather than padded satin stitch; the substantial areas of openwork both in the motifs and round the edge; and the very open nature of this work all suggest a Far-Eastern origin, the Philippines being most noted for this work.*

Plate II.100a (above) *Detail of the pelerine in Plate II.100*
The embroidery includes typically small areas of padded satin stitch and a multitude of eyelets. The edges are formed by rows of contiguous buttonholed eyelets, also suggested in the pattern of 1823 in Plate II.57, p61: similar strings of eyelets occur in several illustrated accessories from the 1810s to early 1830s. The fillings are embroidered inserts of machine net.

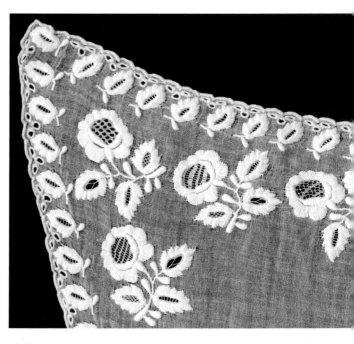

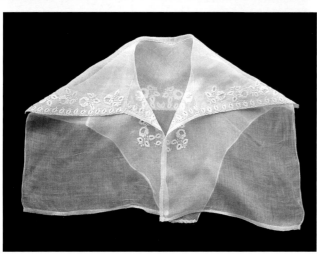

Plate II.101 (opposite bottom left) *Chemisette and collar or pelerine: 1820s or possibly 1830s.*
In wear the collar of this chemisette lies naturally high at the back of the neck and forms a V-shape at the front like many others from the 1820s through into the 1830s. In this position the front edges are almost horizontal with the points of the collar just in front of the shoulders: it thus looks rather like the pelerine in Plate II.95 or the upper layer of Mrs. Powell's pelerine in Plate II.102.

Plate II.101a (opposite top left) *The chemisette in Plate II.101 with the collar flat.*
The almost square front panels and tapered back panel of the chemisette are cut in one piece: the back is on the cross. The small panels of embroidery down the front opening would have shown to advantage in a V-neckline.
Collar: CB - 5⅞in (15cm); Wmax - 20in (50.8cm); side edge - 7¾in (19.7cm); D pattern - 1⅞in (4.8cm)
Chemisette: CB - 12¾ in (32.5cm); CF - 9in (23cm); Back hem - 2in (5cm); Front hem - 10⅝in (27.6cm)

Plate II.101b (opposite top right) *Detail of the chemisette collar in Plate II.101.* The simple, repetitive nature of the embroidery design, with its combination of discrete leaves and curving flower sprays, suggests an 1820s date but the embroidery is unusual: although the fillings are needlepoint lace stitches suggesting an Ayrshire provenance, the dense pattern parts are worked in a combination of padded satin stitch and another stitch which does not feature in Ayrshire work. Needle-lace stitches were also worked on the Continent: perhaps this is of Continental manufacture.

Plate II.101c (opposite bottom right) *Detail of the reverse of the collar in Plate II.101.*

Plate II.102 (above) *Portrait of Mrs. Ann Powell (artist unknown): c.1830: Mercer Art Gallery, Harrogate*
Mrs Powell's double whiteworked pelerine extends over the large sleeve heads of her pink robe and is fastened with a brooch at the neck. Its scalloped edges are decorated with a simple but bold repetitive floral design. This is the first of the larger accessories that we shall see in the following pages. The long lappets hanging down her front are the strings of her elaborate headdress.

Modes de Long Champ

Plate II.103 (left) *Fashion illustration showing 'Modes de Long Champ' for about 1828-29.*

Both ladies wear very elaborate white accessories, that on the left being a 'fichu pelerine' as the pelerine which covers the shoulders extends into long lappets which hang down the front: these are caught under a belt before falling onto the skirt. Fichu pelerines started to appear in fashion plates in about 1826-7. This example has a high neckline surrounded by a ruff which may be a separate accessory.

The canezou worn by the lady on the right has a high neckline with a neat double collar, decorated revers tapering into the waist and flounces over the high sleeve heads. Both ladies' sleeves tighten to the wrists where they are covered by turned-back white cuffs.

In the previous pages we have seen only the mild beginning of the craze for fantastical whiteworked accessories that came to dominate daytime fashion from the late 1820s through into the 1830s. Countless fashion plates record a startling variety of styles from single, wide-spreading pelerines to multi-layered confections with added frills. Wings amplified the width and height of the shoulders: front panels extended into lappets that cascaded onto skirts. All contributed to the frivolous, flamboyant appearance of the period. Only a few examples of these magnificent artefacts can be shown in the following pages.

Plate II.104 (opposite top left) *Fashion illustration from the 'Petit Courrier des Dames' for 1832.*

The two ladies wear different coloured robes but the same particularly extravagant white accessory, showing front and back views: it is described as a 'Canezou de tulle Brodé' (of embroidered net). It includes panels which form large points over the sleeve heads of the dress, yet further panels which form divided wings over these and a vandyked collar which borders the V-shaped front neckline and extends over the shoulders.

The wide shoulder line, the bell-shaped skirt and the V-shaping of the canezou at front and back combine to give the ladies the desired appearance of very slender waists, an illusion exaggerated by the drawing.

Plate II.105 (below right) *Canezou: late 1820s-early 1830s in semi-transparent muslin. This is much more elaborate than the canezou in Plate II.77 and combines features of the accessories in Plates II.103 and II.104. Its main panel tapers in to the waist at front and back where it finishes in very short, plain bands which would be caught under a belt in wear as in Plate II.104. Graduated frills seamed to its outer edges extend from front to back while additional, shorter, wider flounces form wings over full sleeve heads. The semi-circular neckline is finished with a simple standing collar which would most likely have been worn with a ruff like that of the lady in pink in Plate II.103.*

The frills have simple individual flower sprays in each point of the vandyking, not dissimilar to those of Mrs. Powell in Plate II.102: the main panel has a running floral design comparable with the running design in Plate II.88. See p.83 for pattern

Plate II.105a (below left) *Detail from the bottom of the back panel of the canezou in Plate II.105*

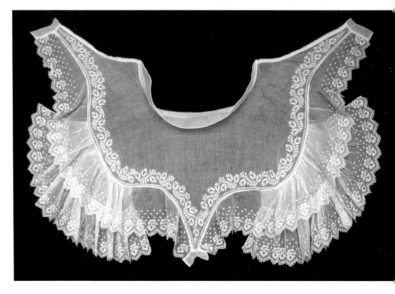

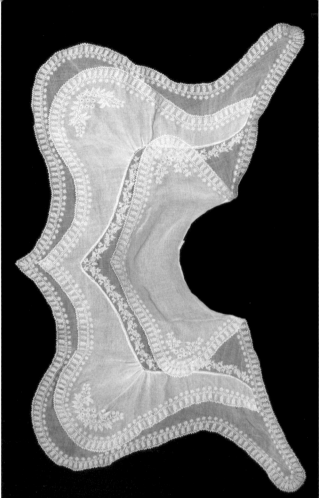

La Mode

*Plate II.106 (left) Detail from a fashion illustration from
'La Mode' for 1832.
The two ladies again wear different coloured robes but the same
accessory to show front and back views.*

*Plate II.107 (above) Fichu pelerine comprising: a main panel which
extends into lappets which would hang down the front of the dress in
wear and might be caught under a belt at the waist; a second layer
sewn onto the main panel at a piped seam and slightly gathered where
it will lie over the shoulders; and a collar.*
*The shape and complexity of this accessory date it definitively to the
late 1820s-mid 1830s but the embroidery is surprisingly simple: it
could easily be mistaken for very early 19th century embroidery but for
the spreading floral motifs over the shoulders. All the motifs are
constituted by minute areas of padded satin stitch with trailing for
lines, overcast eyelets in flower centres and tiny areas of needlepoint
fillings. (See Plate I.30, p23 for detail).*

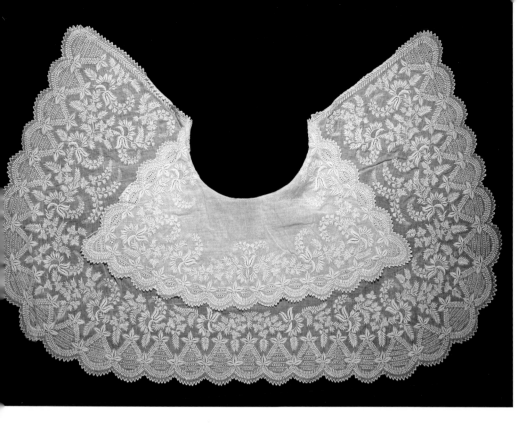

Plate II.108 (left) Double pelerine, early-mid 1830s: St. Fagans, Cat. No. 31-219-16. The two panels of this double pelerine are of different shapes, not an uncommon feature of the period: the design on the lower panel is very carefully drawn to surround the upper panel and not be hidden by it. The pattern on the upper layer is a slightly reduced version of that on the lower layer: both include bold, spreading floral motifs with S-shaped curvature inside scalloped borders with symmetrical, almost geometric designs.
L neck edge - 15½in (39.5cm)
Upper layer: CB - 7in
(17.8cm); Wmax - 35½in
(90cm) Lower layer:
CB - 11¾in (30cm)

Plate II.108a (bottom right)) Detail of the pelerine in Plate II.108.
Although the design covers a much larger proportion of the pelerine than in previous accessories it is still simply but boldly worked in padded satin stitch, trailing and overcast eyelets.

1830-37 WILLIAM IV ON THE THRONE

1830S EARLY DEPARTMENT STORES OR 'BAZAARS'

1830 FIRST SUCCESSFUL CHAIN-STITCH
SEWING MACHINE

1831-36 DARWIN & BEAGLE IN S. AMERICA

1832 REFORM ACT INCREASED FRANCHISE AND
REFORMED PARLIAMENTARY BOROUGHS

1833 BRUNEL APPOINTED TO BUILD THE GREAT WESTERN
RAILWAY; ABOLITION OF SLAVERY IN BRITISH EMPIRE;
FACTORY ACT RESTRICTS WORKING HOURS OF CHILDREN
& YOUNG PERSONS

1834 FIRST LOCK-STITCH SEWING MACHINE;
PALACE OF WESTMINSTER BURNS DOWN

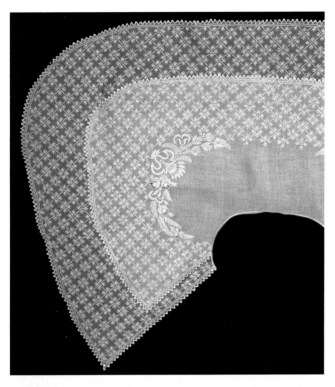

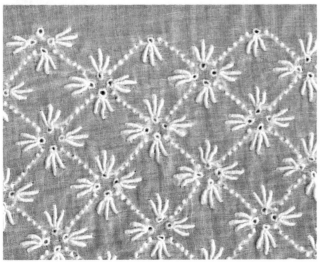

Plate II.109 (top left) *Double pelerine (just over half shown); early-mid 1830s.*

Each layer of this pelerine has a wide border embroidered with a trellis of dotted lines with four triple-leaf sprays at the crossing points: only the spreading floral sprays over the shoulders conform to the designs seen so far in this period but trellis, or diaper, designs became quite popular in the 1830s.

Top layer: CB - 9½in (24cm); Wmax - 27in (69cm)
Bottom layer: CB - 14in (35cm); Wmax - 37in (94cm); neck - 15½in (39cm)

Plate II.109a (top right) *Detail of the pelerine in Plate II.109. The dots are worked with several back stitches, the thread being carried over the back from one stitch to the next.*

Plate II.110 (bottom left) *Detail of a single pelerine of similar shape and size to the larger panel of that in Plate II.109. It has the same trellis design but no floral motifs and the stitching is much less regular betraying this as amateur work.*

Plate II.111 (below) *Double pelerine (just over half shown): early-mid 1830s.*

The size and shape of this pelerine proclaim it to be of roughly the same date as the previous three pelerines illustrated but the embroidery has a lighter character. The floral sprays spread further into the ground from a continuous leafy trail along the edge and denser motifs in padded satin stitch are contrasted with feathery fronds. The edge is finished with tiny buttonholed points outside an openwork band bordered by trailing.

See Plate I.32, p23 for detail.

Top layer: CB - 8½in (21.5cm); Wmax - 27½in (69.7cm); CB pattern - 3¾in (9.5cm) Bottom layer: CB - 14½in (36.8cm); Wmax - 41in (104cm); CB pattern - 6in (15.2cm)

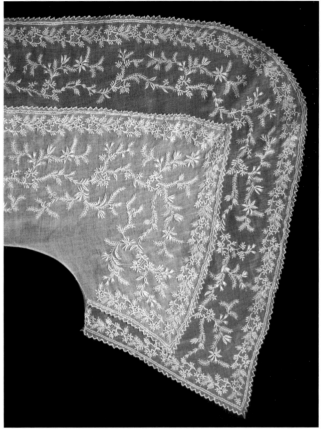

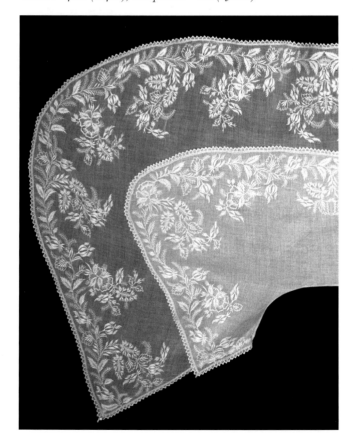

Plate II.112 (above) *Double pelerine (just over half shown): early-mid 1830s.*

Again the size of this pelerine dates it to the early-mid 1830s but the design of meandering, branching trails is very different from previous ones. It shows the desire in the 1830s to get away from the small, repetitive floral designs of previous decades. It is, however, worked in typical stitches for the period: padded satin stitch for the tiny leaves and petals, trailing for the stems, and some pulled fillings and overcast eyelets.

Top layer: CB - 15in (38cm); Wmax - 25¾in (65.5cm); L front edge - 5¼in (13.3cm) Bottom layer: CB - 8½in (21.5cm); Wmax - 35¼in (89.5cm); L front edge - 10in (25.5cm)

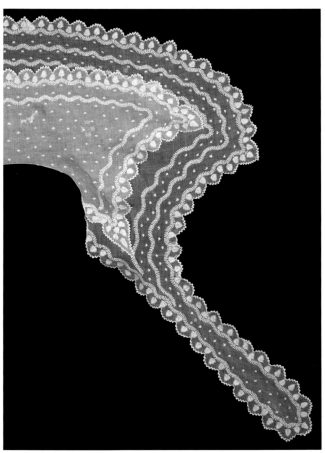

Plate II.114 (above) *Double fichu pelerine (just over half shown): mid-1830s.*

The 'Journal des Demoiselles' for 1835 includes a pattern for a pelerine of almost exactly the same shape as this but with a slightly shallower back. This pelerine gains its attraction from the delicacy of its fabric which would drape naturally over the large sleeves of the period and the contrast between its dense embroidery and the transparency of the muslin.

Top layer: L neck edge - 14in (35.5cm); CB - 7½in (19cm); Wmax - 19½in (49.5cm) Bottom layer - CB - 9½in (24cm); Wmax - 23in (58.5cm)

Plate II.113 (above) *Portrait of a lady: The Mercer Art Gallery, Harrogate: c.mid 1830s*

This unknown lady wears a double pelerine with deeply vandyked edges loosely round her shoulders. The white embroidery shows beautifully against the transparent muslin.

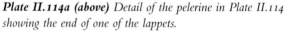

Plate II.114a (above) *Detail of the pelerine in Plate II.114 showing the end of one of the lappets.*
Only padded satin stitch and trailing are used for the design. The scalloped edge is worked in graduated buttonhole stitch, or 'scalloping', giving a very strong outline. Were it not for this edging, the simple embroidery design, which includes a laurel trail, would suggest a much earlier date for this pelerine than is possible given its shape and size.

Plate II.114b (top right) *The pelerine in Plate II.114 as in wear.*

Plate II.115 (bottom right) *Detail from a mid-1830s fashion plate showing a complex fichu pelerine. The shoulder line tends to be wider rather than higher by 1835 but collars still ride high at the back of the neck. Small collars such as that incorporated in the pelerine could still be worn as separate accessories as demonstrated by the collar with a double-frilled edge shown below.*

Cuffs

Before continuing with collars and pelerines we shall make a brief digression. During the 1820s the changes in bodice and skirt shapes were accompanied by changes in sleeve length: full-length sleeves had been very long, covering the backs of the hands in earlier years, but they now shortened to the wrist where they were often finished with tight cuffs. This new style lent itself to the addition of cuffs that turned back over the sleeve fabric: these might be of the dress fabric itself but might alternatively be of whitework, in which case they might match the decoration of a pelerine, chemisette, or other accessory. In the late 1820s - mid 1830s this resulted in cuffs that were as flamboyant as the accessory they matched but, in the later 1830s, they became smaller and neater. The following plates show several examples from the late 1820s–1830s: a few more cuffs will also be illustrated in later pages.

See p100 for patterns of several cuffs on pp96-99.

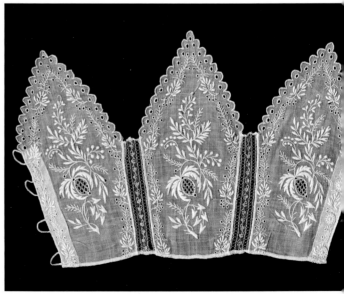

Plate II.116 (above) Detail from a fashion illustration of 1830.
The lady wears a white pelerine with a collar and small neck ruff.
White vandyked cuffs turn back over the dress sleeves. (Not all cuffs
of the period turned back.) (Harris M & AG)

Plate II.117 (right) Cuff: late 1820s-early 1830s.
The three vandyked panels are joined by bobbin lace insertions.
The embroidery resembles that of the accessories in Plates II.63 and
II.74 in its delicacy. It includes lightly-padded satin stitch, trailing,
overcast eyelets and pulled-thread fillings. It fastens with four
mother-of-pearl buttons and buttonholed loops.
Wmax - 9¾in (24.5cm); D into point - 6in (15cm)

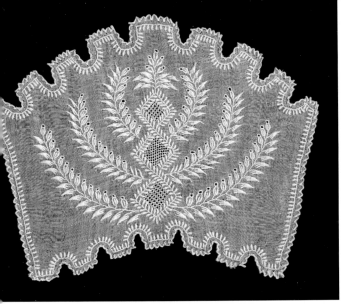

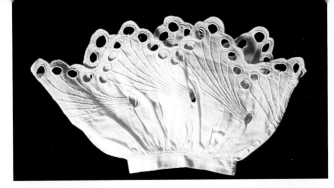

Plate II.118 (above left) *Cuff: late 1820s-early 1830s.*
The unusual outline of this cuff matches the flamboyance of many
pelerines of the period.

Plate II.119 (top right) *Cuff: late 1820s-early 1830s:*
Hereford M & AG.
Although the design of this cuff is simple and non-floral, its
boldness and asymmetry mark it as a product of the 1820s-1830s.

Plate II.120 (middle right)
Cuff: late 1820s-early 1830s:
Hereford M & AG, Cat. No.
7259/4.

Plate II.121 (bottom right)
Cuff: probably late 1820s-early
1830s. This cuff is more difficult
to date: its central neo-classical
design in satin stitch rather than
padded satin stitch suggests an
early 19th century date but the
flamboyance of the deep,
gathered lace frill suggests the
1820s-1830s.

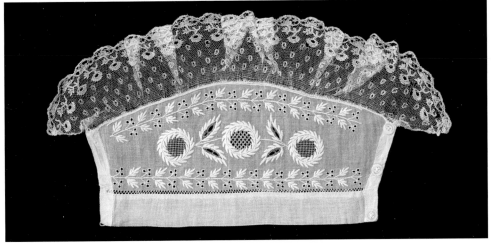

Plate II.122 (right) *Cuff: late 1820s-early 1830s*
The embroidery on the two parts of this cuff show that one panel turns up and the other down. The edges are beautifully worked in scalloping - see Plates I.7, 7a, p11, for details.

Plate II.122a (above) *The cuff in Plate II.122 as in wear*

Plate II.123 (right) *Cuff: late 1820s-early 1830s*

Plate II.124 (above) *Cuff: probably 1830s. The use of outlined padded satin stitch and the filling of the ground with a branching pattern suggest that this dates from the late 1830s rather than earlier.*

Plate II.125 (top right) *Cuff: probably 1830s: Hereford M & AG, Cat. No. 7259/11*
This is made in a combination of fine muslin and a dense cotton piqué fabric.

Plate II.126 (middle right) *Cuff: probably mid 1830s. Hereford M & AG, Cat. No.7259-5.*
This shows another version of a trellis design: it has outlined padded satin stitch spots at the corners.

Plate II.127 (bottom right) *Cuff: probably late 1830s. This has an extra panel of plain muslin added to the wrist band as shown in the pattern on p100.*

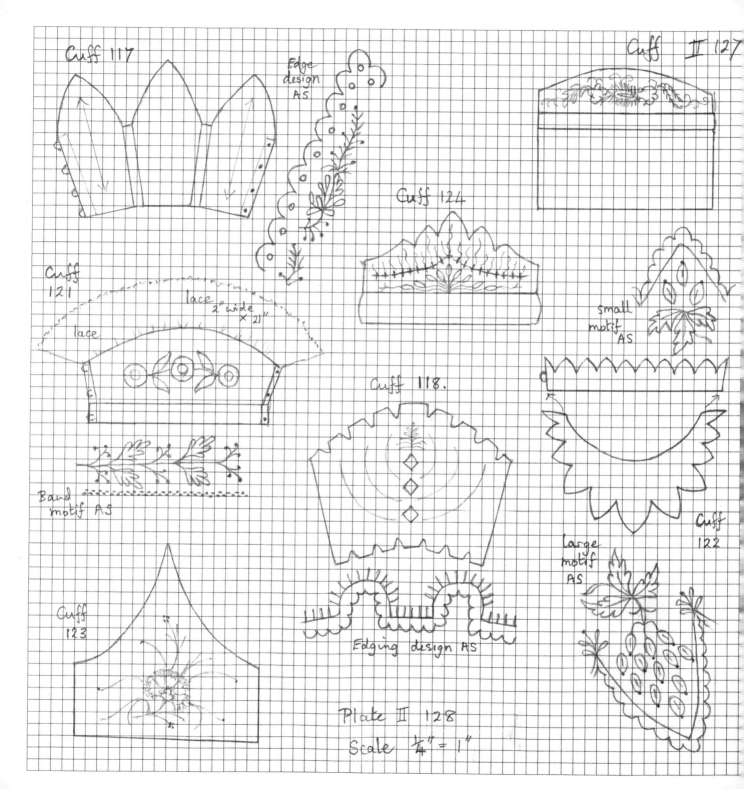

Cuff 117

Edge design AS

Cuff II 127

Cuff 124

Cuff 121

lace 2" wide × 21"

lace

small motif AS

Band motif AS

Cuff 118.

Cuff 122

large motif AS

Cuff 123

Edging design AS

Plate II 128

Scale ¼" = 1"

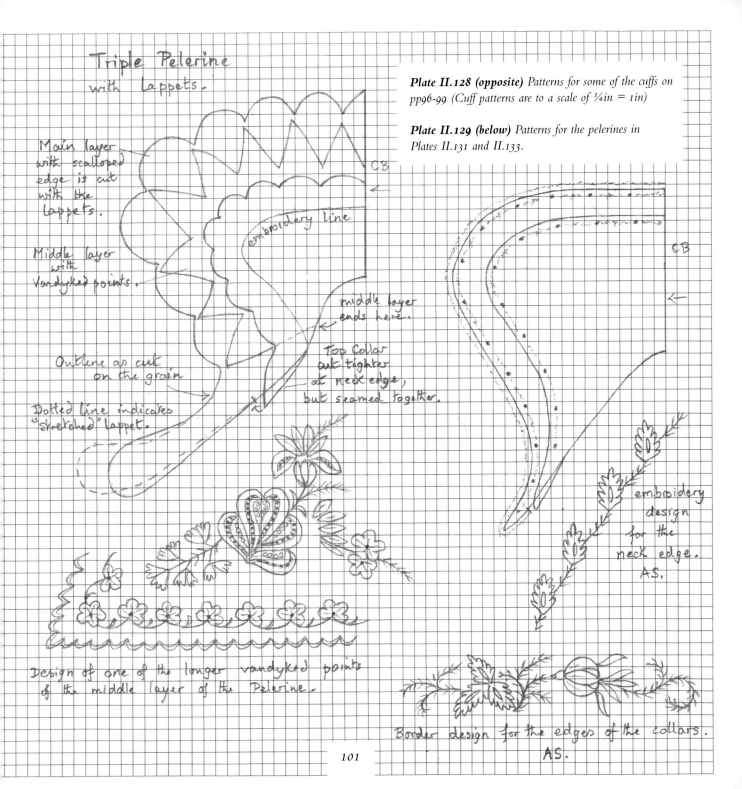

Triple Pelerine
with Lappets.

Main layer with scalloped edge is cut with the lappets.

Middle layer with Vandyked points.

Outline as cut on the grain

Dotted line indicates "stretched" lappet.

embroidery line

CB

middle layer ends here.

Top Collar cut tighter at neck edge, but seamed together.

Design of one of the longer vandyked points of the middle layer of the Pelerine.

Plate II.128 (opposite) *Patterns for some of the cuffs on pp96-99 (Cuff patterns are to a scale of ¼in = 1in)*

Plate II.129 (below) *Patterns for the pelerines in Plates II.131 and II.133.*

CB

embroidery design for the neck edge. AS.

Border design for the edges of the collars. AS.

THE MID TO LATE 1830s
A few more pelerines and fichus

Most of the large pelerines shown so far have roughly semi-circular necklines which would fit closely round the neck in wear and this appears to be the most common form in the late 1820s–mid 1830s but more open V-necklines are occasionally seen in illustrations: the doll in Plates II.130–II.130c, for example, has one canezou with a round neckline and one with a V-neckline. From the mid 1830s the V-neckline appears to become the more common form. The next few pelerines probably date from the middle of the decade as they are extremely wide and would need the support of huge sleeves in wear but have almost smoothly-curved necklines and other features that were introduced gradually during the 1830s.

Published by R. ACKERMANN, JUN.ᴿ 191 Regent St.ᵗ
Sold also at 96 Strand.

Plates II.130, II.130a (above and top right) *Front and partial back views of a paper doll wearing a striped dress and an elaborate canezou with a wide pelerine edged with a gathered frill, extra flounces over the very full dress sleeves and an open V-neckline: early 1830s. The doll has several other interchangeable outfits, one of which is also shown here, but, unfortunately, has lost her hat/hats.*

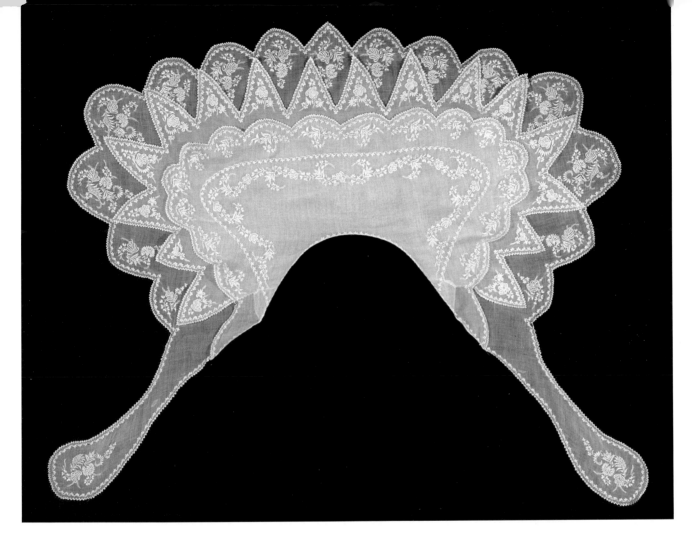

Plate II.131 *A triple fichu pelerine: early-mid 1830s. This particularly fantastic example of a fichu pelerine has three deeply vandyked and scalloped layers and long lappets: such extravaganzas were worn into the mid 1830s. Different bold floral sprays fill the scallops and points of the three layers inside a very simple running floral border: the top layer also has a repeat of the running border outside a more complex running design and a plain centre. See p101 for pattern and Plate I.29, p22 for a detail.*
CB: top layer - 8in (20cm); middle layer - 9½in (24cm); bottom layer (into centre point) - 15¾in (40cm) Wmax: top - 28in (71cm); middle - 37½in (95cm); bottom - 41½in (105.5cm) L lappet (from join with top layer) - 16¼in (41.5cm)

Plates II.130b (opposite right middle), II.130c (opposite bottom right)
Partial front and back views of the doll in Plate II.130 wearing a different floral-print dress and whiteworked canezou. The canezou includes a vandyked collar with a round neckline, a vandyked flounce seamed to the body of the canezou to simulate a pelerine and added flounces with square vandyking over the sleeves. The embroidered decoration is more complex than that of the doll's other canezou.

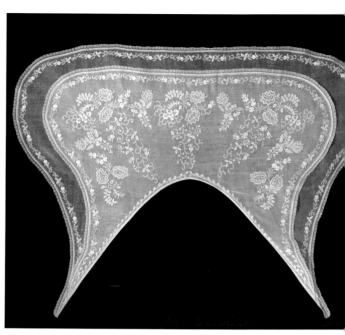

Plate II.133 (above) *Double fichu pelerine; mid 1830s.*
This, though not the most elaborate of the pelerines shown so far, is the widest. Its two layers are seamed together at a smoothly curved neckline and extend into points at the front. They naturally form a V-neckline when worn. The outer edges, also smoothly curved, are trimmed with a Valenciennes bobbin lace. The narrow bands of floral patterning inside this do not flow continuously but comprise repeated, elongate sprays with solidly-worked flowers interspersed with finer, curling fronds. The main design, solely on the upper layer, includes a wide floral band of similar character from which three lighter sprays extend in narrow triangles towards the neckline. The contrasts in the embroidery and the spreading nature of the design are characteristics which appear to enter the embroiderers' repertoire in the early 1830s and gradually become more common through into the second half of the decade. See p101 for pattern
Top layer - L neck edge - 37½in (94.5cm); Wmax - 35½in (90cm); CB 11¼in (28.5cm); Wmax - 31¾in (80.5cm)
Bottom layer - CB - 13½in (24cm); Wmax - 38½in (98cm); D lace - ⅜in (1cm)

Plate II.132 (above) *Fashion illustration of about 1835.*
Here the dress sleeves have enormous width but have lost the exaggerated height of earlier years so that the double fichu pelerine falls in a smooth line over the shoulders. The edges of both layers of the pelerine are gently curved and bordered by a simple running design. The entire upper layer is patterned: floral motifs spread from the outer border and occupy ovals near the neckline.

Plate II.133a (below) *Detail of the pelerine in Plate II.133. The embroidery is superbly executed: the complex leaves and flowers are worked in carefully shaped padded satin stitch and contrasted with a background of curling fronds in trailing. Fillings are in pulled-thread, spot and ladder stitches.*

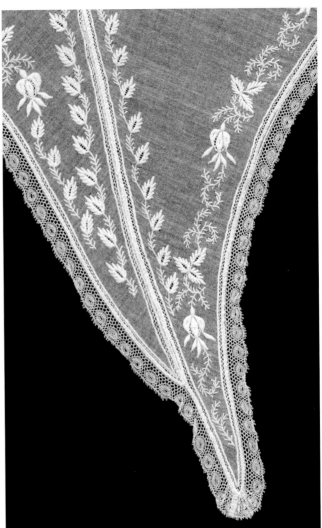

Plate II.133b (above) *Further detail of the pelerine in Plate II.133 showing the neck seam opened flat.*
Each side of the seam is finished with a line of buttonholing, a drawn or pulled line and a trailed line: the outer edge of each layer is finished in the same way. A simple leaf pattern runs along each side of the seam.

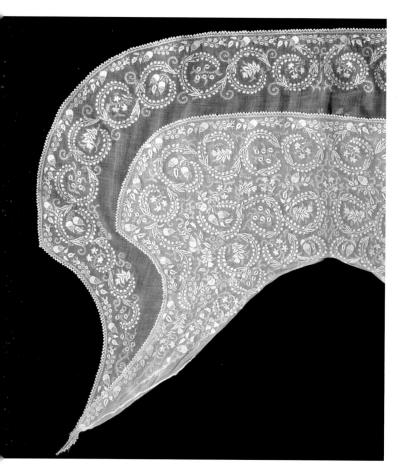

Plate II.134a (below) *A detail from the pelerine in Plate II.134. The design may be unusual but the stitching is typical of the 1830s: it includes veined and indented padded satin stitch, ladder-stitch veins and trailed lines, some forming a feathery background. The delightful acorns are in diapered satin stitch and backstitched dots. The edge is scalloped outside a line of openwork between trailed lines.*

Plate II.134 (above) *Double pelerine (just over half shown); mid 1830s. This has a similar neckline to the previous example but a different outline: the embroidery is not so accomplished. The design is unusual for the period but accords with the general desire for novelty in the 1830s: it is based on late Elizabethan/Jacobean designs - see Plate II.135 - but its scrolls, enclosed sprays, and the decoration between them are more complex than in the originals and in very different embroidery stitches.*

Top layer: CB - 10in (25.5cm); Wmax - 29in (73.5cm)
Bottom: CB - 15½in (39.3cm); Wmax - 39in (99cm)
Neck edge 46in (117cm): W tip-to-tip - 39½in (101cm)

The pelerines in Plates II.131-II.132 show the final stages in the growth of the pelerine. By 1835 sleeve heads were starting to lose their height and were to grow no wider. By 1836 their fullness had started to slip down the arm: they could no longer support the wide pelerines of previous years. These first draped loosely over the puffs and frills on the upper arms but their width soon reduced and gradually their shaping changed to complement the evolving silhouette of the female form.

It took some time for these changes to spread throughout society: large sleeves and correspondingly extravagant accessories continued to be worn into the later 1830s despite the dictates of fashion magazines. It is therefore impossible to give a true cut-off date for the huge pelerines of the late 1820s-1830s but change did creep in and the following pages will show the nature of this change even if they cannot be true to the actual timescale.

Plate II.135 *Detail from an early 17th century linen coif decorated with silk and metal thread embroidery in a typical scrolling design of the period.*

Plate II.136 *Detail from a fashion illustration of 1835 showing 'Morning dresses'. This is of about the same date as the illustration in Plate II.132 but the pelerines form a more decidedly conical line over the shoulders.*

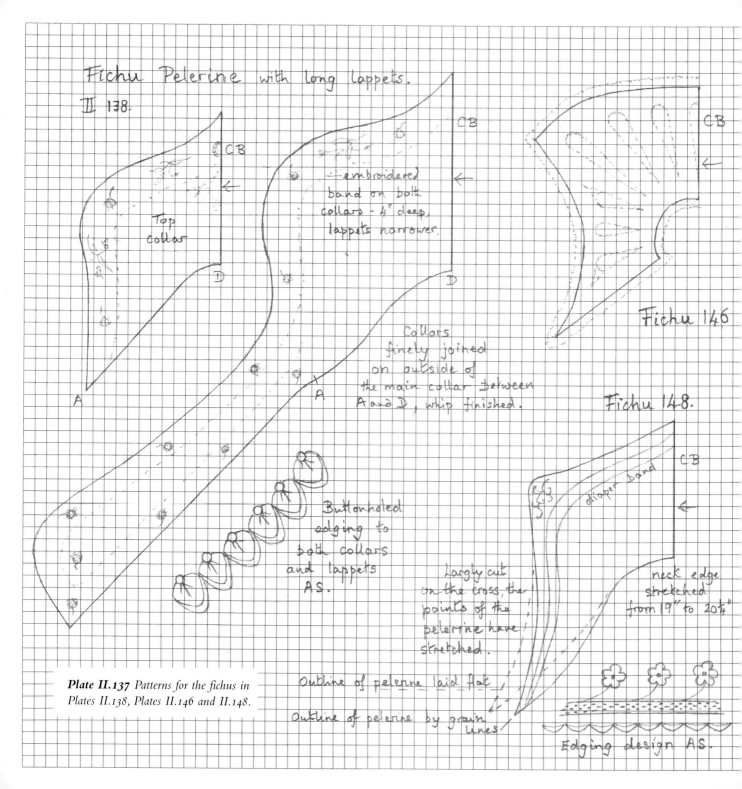

Fichu Pelerine with long lappets.
II 138.

CB

Top collar

CB

embroidered band on both collars - 4" deep, lappets narrower.

CB

D

D

Fichu 146

A

A

Collars finely joined on outside of the main collar between A and D, whip finished.

Fichu 148.

CB

diaper band

Buttonholed edging to both collars and lappets A.S.

Largely cut on the cross, the points of the pelerine have stretched.

neck edge stretched from 19" to 20½"

Plate II.137 Patterns for the fichus in Plates II.138, Plates II.146 and II.148.

Outline of pelerine laid flat

Outline of pelerine by grain lines

Edging design A.S.

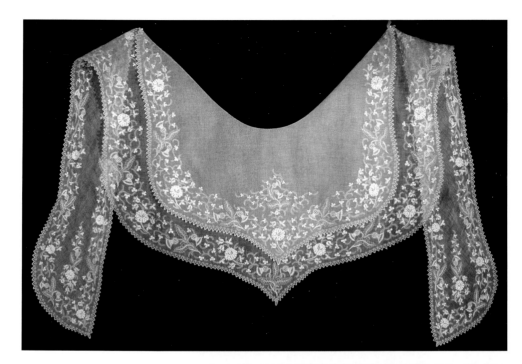

Plate II.138 (left) *Double fichu or fichu pelerine: 1837? The outline of this accessory is very similar to that of a magazine pattern of 1836 (not illustrated): the embroidery style is also commensurate with a date in the later 1830s. The reason for suggesting a specific date of 1837 is the inclusion of roses, shamrocks and thistles in its design: a collar shown in Plate II.160 has similar motifs and also the name 'Victoria' under a crown: I suggest that both of these accessories were made to celebrate Queen Victoria's coronation in 1837.*

Plate II.138a (right) *Detail of a lappet of the fichu in Plate II.138 showing the rose, thistle and shamrock design. The elongate triangles of decoration seen in the lappets were very fashionable in the later 1830s-early 1840s: an example dated 1840 is seen in Plate II.147. The embroidery style in which bold padded satin stitch motifs were set against a lighter, feathery background was popular in the mid-late 1830s but was gradually being superseded by other styles.*

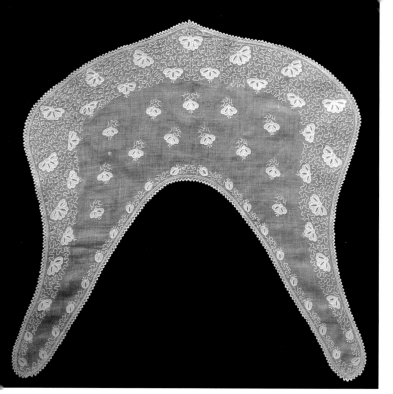

Plate II.139 (above) *Fichu: mid-late 1830s.*
Here is fichu with an outline similar to that of the fichu in Plate II.138 apart from the long lappets but with very different embroidery. The dense motifs are created by appliqué work.

Plate II.139a (above) *Detail of the fichu in Plate II.139. The two layers of fabric in the dense motifs are sewn together with buttonhole stitch. Those in the outer band are set against a light ground of trailed vermicular lines, a less common alternative to the feathery fronds seen in the previous fichu.*

Plate II.140 (left) *Cuff: mid-late 1830s. The flower heads and leaves of this design are set against a combination of twiggy and vermicular lines. Unusually, all are worked in heavily-padded satin stitch within an outline of buttonholed rings.*

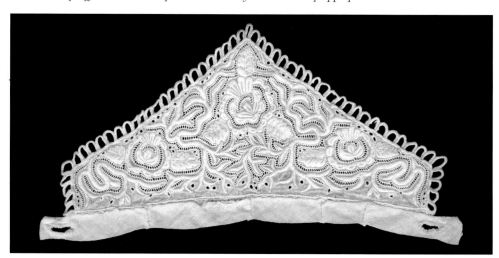

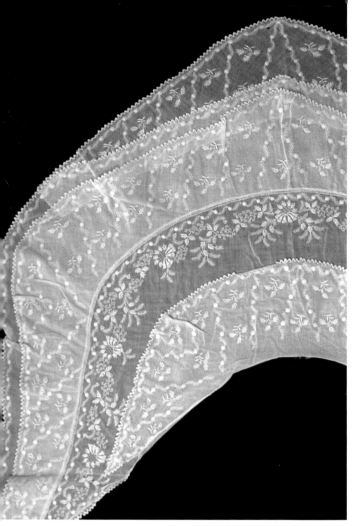

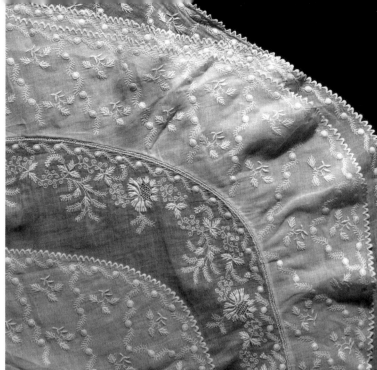

Plate II.141 (top left) *Complex fichu pelerine; late 1830s-early 1840s: The Museum of Fashion, Blandford Forum.*
The outline of this fichu pelerine is again similar to that of the fichu pelerine in Plate II.139. Its main panel gives the overall shape and also supports a collar, a shaped flounce which extends from the front points right round the back, and an additional narrow border applied beneath the flounce but only across the back.

Plate II.141a (above) *Detail of the fichu pelerine in Plate II.141. An interesting feature of this fichu is its linear decoration which has parallels in a collar in Plate II.152 below. The embroidery also includes a band of floral sprays in contrasting dense and feathery stitches similar to that of a collar pattern of 1839 in Plate II.145, p113.*

Plate II.142 (left) *Detail from a fashion illustration of 1836. Here the sleeve fullness has already slipped from the shoulders onto the upper arms. An accessory that the text describes as a 'fichu' is shown in front and back views: the fichus in Plates II.139 and II.140 would probably have been worn in a similar manner, close round the shoulders with their ends crossed in front.*

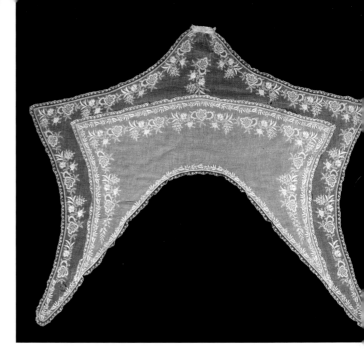

Plate II.144a (opposite, top left) *The fichu in Plate II.144 as in wear. The embroidery comprises discrete floral motifs that form a continuous band of decoration which is extremely similar in character to that of the collar pattern of 1839 in Plate II.145, even to the taper at the ends. The lower back has a short hem indicating that this part would be concealed by a belt but, surprisingly, it has an embroidered sprig just above the hem. Upper layer - L neck edge - 37½in (94.5cm); CB - 11¼ in (28.5cm); Wmax - 35½in (90cm) Lower layer - CB - 13½in (24cm); Wmax - 38½in (98cm)*

Plate II.143 (top left) *Fashion illustration of about 1836-9 (Harris M & AG). Both ladies wear the newly fashionable style of evening bodice with a very sloping shoulder line and puffs and frills round the upper arms. The three white fichus have correspondingly sloping shoulder lines and tapered ends that cross over at the front to form V-shaped necklines: their borders are slightly wavy or frilled but no longer deeply vandyked.*

Plate II.144 (top right) *Double fichu: mid-late 1830s. The exaggerated points and convexly-curved edges of this double fichu would sit very neatly over the sloping shoulder line of the late 1830s as seen in Plate II.143.*

Plate II.144b (opposite, top right) *Detail of the double fichu in Plate II.144. The outer and neck edges are buttonholed and bordered by lines of pulled or drawn work between trailed lines and a very narrow (³⁄₈in - 1cm) Buckinghamshire point bobbin lace.*

Plate II.145 (opposite bottom) *Page of patterns from a 'Journal des Demoiselles' of 1839. The main pattern is for a collar that is smaller than the fichu in Plate II.121 but has a similar embroidery design. Other features are border patterns and a handkerchief corner with the goose and fox from one of Aesop's fables. Note the geometric centres to the motifs in the left-hand border and in the square at the top: geometric features often occur in late 1830s-early 1840s designs.*

Journal des Demoiselles.

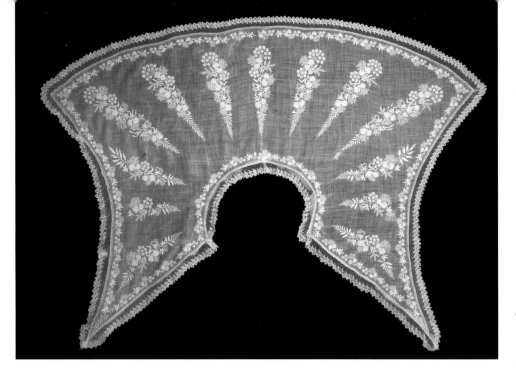

Plate II.146 (left, top)

*Fichu: probably late 1830s.
See p108 for pattern and
Plate I.36, p25 for detail.
This has concavely curved sides
like those of the fichu in Plate
II.144 but a smooth back curve
and part-circular neckline which
would probably have been
closed round the neck in wear.
The elongate triangles of
decoration have similar outlines
to those of the fichu pelerine in
Plate II.138 but their massed
flower heads and leaves give a
rather different impression, more
like the crowded designs in the
pattern of 1840 in Plate II.147.
They are beautifully graduated
to fit the shape of the fichu.
CF - 11in + 1in lace (28cm +
2.5cm)
Wmax - 30in including lace
(76cm)
Neck edge - 14½in (37cm)*

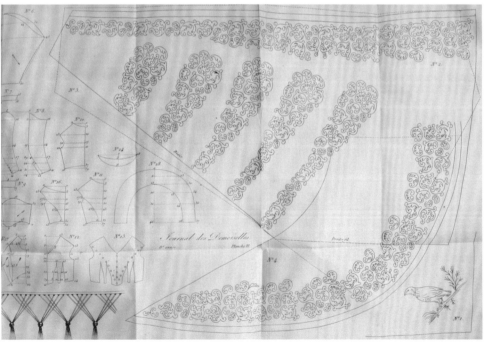

Plate II.147 (opposite bottom) *Page of patterns from the 'Journal des Demoiselles' of June 1840. This page includes a pattern for a 'fichu-canezou; pattern No.2 is for half the front, No.3 for half the back and No.4 for the collar. The elongate triangles of decoration give a similar effect to those on the fichu in Plate II.146 despite the fact that they consist of masses of C-shaped scrolls. Such scrolls are frequently employed in rococo decoration, a major influence in embroidery designs in the 1830s-40s. This, like several other patterns illustrated, was printed on yellow paper*

Plate II.148 (top left) *Mid-late 1830s fichu (just over half shown). This fichu includes features of shape and floral decoration which are clearly similar to those of several fichus already illustrated but also includes a more unusual diaper band sandwiched between the floral designs.*

Plate II.148a (top right) *Detail of the fichu in Plate II.148. The diaper band comprises lines of openwork (probably pulled) between two parallel trailed lines. The work is meticulous.*

Collars and smaller pelerines (mid 1830s to early 1840s)

The huge pelerines and later fichus seen in previous pages complemented the fashions of their periods but, at the same time, smaller collars or pelerines that fell onto but did not cover the shoulders were still worn. These might form upper layers on other accessories, as already seen on a few pelerines and chemisettes, or might be separate items, but their shapes were not so governed by the style of the underlying dress as those of larger items. Their necklines and outer edges were therefore very varied and did not change in a logical progression. A look at 'The Workwoman's Guide' published in 1837 and 1840 shows numerous different shapes in a single page of patterns.

How surviving collars looked when worn is not always easy to tell: they usually comprise flat panels of fabric that do not sit neatly round a curved neckline. Fashion illustrations, such as that in Plate II.149, do, however, confirm that they might look creased in wear. Moreover, their front edges may but need not meet at the front or, if pointed, may be crossed over each other.

Plate II.149 (above) Detail from a fashion illustration of 1832-33. The lady's collar, worn high around her neck, clearly shows crease marks. This probably shows the reality of fashion as many surviving collars comprise flat panels of fabric which, though having curved necklines, do not sit happily round the curvature of the neck.

*Plate II.150 (left) Detail of a collared chemisette; mid-late 1830s: Walker M & AG: Cat. No.1970.100.1
The chemisette is shown as in wear: the depth of the collar falling behind the shoulders can just be seen.*

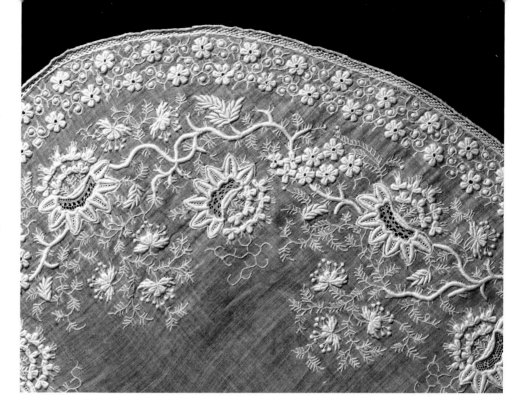

For help with dating we must look to changes in embroidery styles. As already seen in the pelerines, designs in the late 1820s tended to consist mainly of bold floral motifs in padded satin stitch and trailing but, by the mid 1830s, bold motifs were often set against lighter backgrounds.

As the decade wore on, greater varieties of stitch and motif were introduced but even the combination of shape and embroidery does not allow close dating.

Plate II.150a (above) Detail of the collar of the chemisette in Plate II.150. A narrow border surrounds a deeper design, all worked in heavily padded satin stitch against lighter fronds and curling tendrils. A stem runs through the design but is broken and branching unlike the sinuous trails of the early 19th century. Although deep designs were fashionable, the narrow border on its own would have been acceptable: fashion magazines specifically stated that the inner border need not be worked if the embroiderers did not have time. The satin stitch includes veined and outlined versions: fine lines are in whipped running, fillings in needlepoint lace typical of the best Ayrshire work.

Plate II.151 (right) Small pelerine or large collar: mid-late 1830s. Discrete floral motifs spread along the border, almost touching but not merging with each other. Dense pattern areas in padded satin stitch contrast with feathery fronds in whipped running: the design is very similar to that of the collar pattern of 1839 in Plate II.145 even though the collar shape is not. See Plate I.33, p24 for a detail CB - 10¾in (27.3cm); Wmax - 26in (66cm)

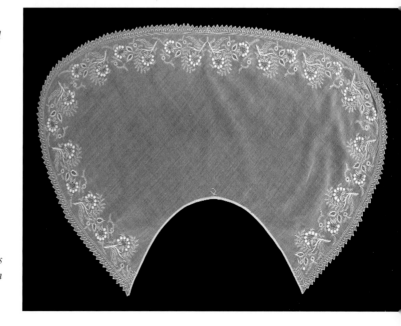

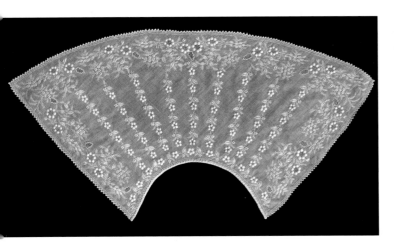

Plate II.152 (above) Small pelerine or collar: mid-late 1830s. This example has a very different outline from the pelerines seen previously but its lines of decoration radiating from the neck are reminiscent of those in the fichu in Plate II.141. See p119 for pattern

Plate II.152a (above right) Detail of the pelerine in Plate II.152. The radial lines consist of repeated, small discrete sprigs but, leaving aside the overall design, these cannot be confused with the simple sprigs of the early 1800s-1820s because of the way they are embroidered in a combination of bold and feathery stitching. The neck edge of this particular pelerine is hemmed and very finely worked with overstitching.

Plate.II.153 (left) Detail of the border of a pelerine or collar of similar shape, date and embroidery style to that in Plate II.151. The unusual geometric feature of the design has an equivalent in a border pattern of 1839 in Plate II.145.

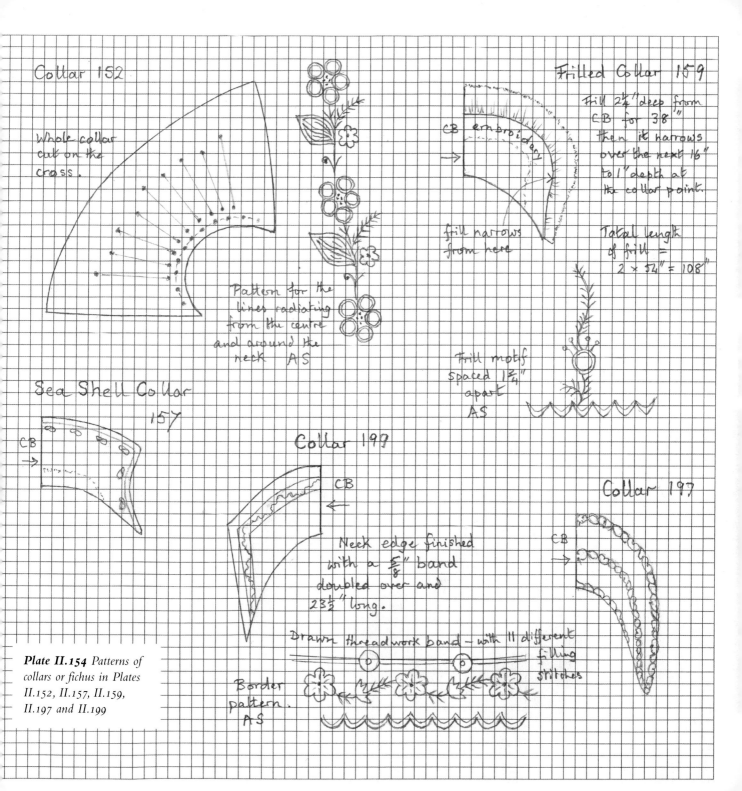

Collar 152

Whole collar cut on the cross.

Pattern for the lines radiating from the centre and around the neck AS

Sea Shell Collar 157

CB

Collar 199

CB

Neck edge finished with a $\frac{5}{8}$" band doubled over and $23\frac{1}{2}$" long.

Drawn threadwork band — with 11 different filling stitches

Border pattern. AS

Frilled Collar 159

CB embroidery

Fill $2\frac{1}{4}$" deep from CB for 38" then it narrows over the next 16" to 1" depth at the collar point.

Total length of frill = $2 \times 54" = 108"$

frill narrows from here

Frill motifs spaced $1\frac{3}{4}$" apart AS

Collar 199

CB

Plate II.154 *Patterns of collars or fichus in Plates II.152, II.157, II.159, II.197 and II.199*

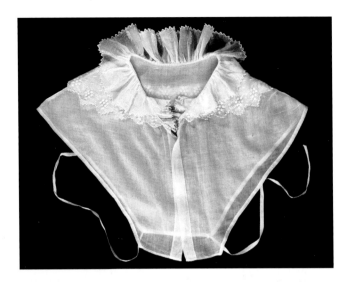

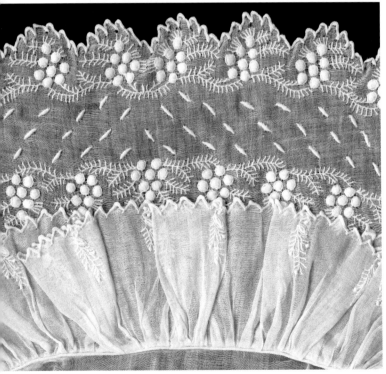

Plate II.155 (top left) *Collared chemisette with a ruff; 1830s.*
In contrast to the collars in Plates II.150-II.153, the collar of this chemisette has a very simple repetitive design. All three panels of the chemisette are cut on the straight: the shoulder seams are piped, as is the seam joining the chemisette body, collar and ruff.
A draw string is held in a casing at the lower back: there is no sign of fastening at the front.
Chemisette: CB - 12in (30.5cm); front edges - 9½in (24cm)
Collar: CB - 5¾in (14.6cm); neck - 18¾in (47.7cm)
Ruff: Dmax - 2½in (6.3cm)

Plate II.155a (top right) *Detail of the collar and ruff of the chemisette in Plate II.155.*
The collar includes two bands of floral decoration separated by a spot pattern. The flowing feathery stem in whipped running carries groups of eight berries worked in outlined padded satin stitch.
The scalloped edge is worked in very simple buttonhole stitches.

Plate II.155b (bottom left) *Closer detail of the ruff and collar of the chemisette in Plate II.155. The neck ruffle is decorated with narrow, isolated, floral motifs that extend from the outer edge towards the neckline. Similar patterning is seen on many ruffs and ruffles added to the edges of accessories dating from the 1830s-40s: a specific example (not shown) is given in the Journal des Demoiselles for 1836.*

1836 DICKENS' PICKWICK PAPERS SERIALISED

1837 VICTORIA BECOMES QUEEN; 1ST DAGUERROTYPE PRODUCED; MORSE PATENTS THE TELEGRAPH

1838 REGULAR UK – US STEAMSHIP SERVICE STARTED; GRACE DARLING'S RESCUE OF SHIPWRECK VICTIMS OFF FARNE ISLANDS

1839 1ST EDN. OF BRADSHAW'S RAILWAY TIMETABLE; BELGIUM'S INDEPENDENCE GUARANTEED; GOODYEAR VULCANISES RUBBER

Plate II.156 (above) Detail of the corner of a double pelerine: mid-late 1830s. Hampshire collection: Cat. No.1966.493. The border design includes narrow motifs extending away from the edge like those in the ruff in Plate II.156 though these are slightly bolder and grow from a simple border trail.

Plate II.157 (right) Collar or pelerine: mid-late 1830s (just over half shown). See p119 for pattern. This has an extraordinary design of seashells against a background of feathery fronds. By the 1830s many designers and their public had tired of small repetitive floral patterns and looked for inspiration to all sorts of works, whether ancient designs or the latest scientific treatises. Exotic designs such as this were welcomed. Fillings are insertions of embroidered net.
CB - 5⅝in (14.5cm);
Wmax - 17in (43cm).

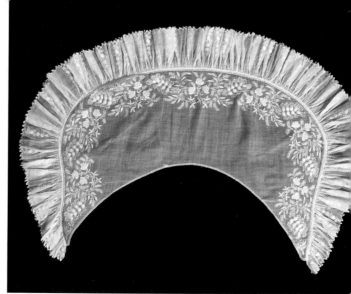

Plate II.159 (above) *Small frilled collar or fichu: late 1830s. The floral border has a more delicate character than most designs seen so far. It is completely filled with patterning. The frill is beautifully gathered and tapers at the sides. It is decorated with isolated, narrow floral motifs that extend from the outer edge towards the neckline like those of the ruff in Plate II.155. Main panel: Wmax - 15in (38cm); CB - 5¼ in (13cm) Frill: Dmax - 2¼in (5.8cm)*

Plate II.159a (below) *The collar in Plate II.159 shown as in wear. See page 119 for pattern*

Plate II.158 (above) *Detail from a fashion illustration of 1838. The bodice shows the new dress fashion for sleeve fullness lower down the arms. Lower necklines also became more popular in daywear at this time. The diaper pattern of the fabric has already been seen in a pelerine (Plate II.109) and is often seen in 1830s-40s fabrics. The collar or fichu worn here could be carried by a chemisette or could be a separate entity like that in Plate II.159.*

Plate II.160 (right) *Small frilled collar or fichu: probably 1837.*
This much loved and darned fichu or collar bears the name 'Victoria' beneath a crown together with roses, thistles and shamrocks representing England, Scotland and Ireland. Its general shape and embroidery style date it to the late 1830s-early 1840s: the patriotic motifs strongly suggest that it was made to celebrate Queen Victoria's coronation in 1837 although her wedding in 1841 is a possible alternative. The frill is of Buckinghamshire point bobbin lace.
Main panel:
Wmax - 15in (38cm);
CB - 5in (12.6cm).
Frill: D - 1¼in (3.3cm)

Plate II.160a (right) *Detail of the collar in Plate II.160. Some dense areas of design are created by padded satin stitch, others by an applied second layer of fabric. Stitching is worked over both single and double layers of the fabric.*

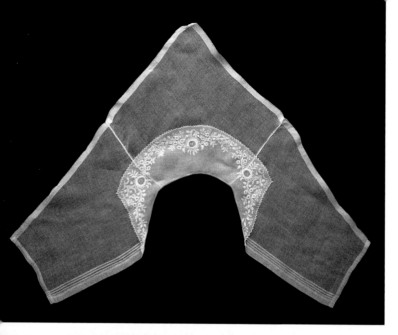

Plate II.161 (top left) *Collared chemisette; probably late 1830s-early 1840s. The chemisette body is formed from three panels joined at the shoulders at piped seams, a common feature of fine sewing from the later 1820s although seen earlier. The back panel is cut on the cross, the fronts on the straight. The linear bands of decoration down the front edges are formed in the weave and by a hem. Chemisette: CB - 15½in (39.4cm); CF - 11½in (29.2cm); shoulder seam - 5½in (14cm). Collar: CB - 4¾in (12cm); front edge - 6¾in (17.3cm); neck - 20in (51cm)*

Plate II.161a (bottom left *Detail of the collar of the chemisette in Plate II.161. The collar of this example is decorated with only three floral motifs which spread from the corners and centre back and are worked in padded satin stitch with light feathery fronds and curling tendrils in whipped running. The three large fillings are of pulled-thread work and the small ones of needlepoint lace.*

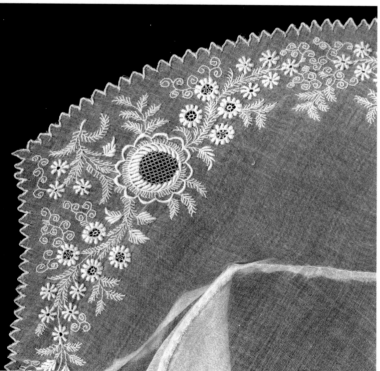

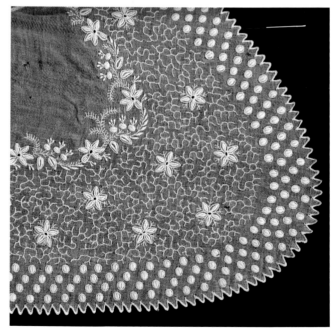

Plate II.162a (above) *Detail of the pelerine of the chemisette in Plate II.162. See Plate I.31, p23 for a close detail.*

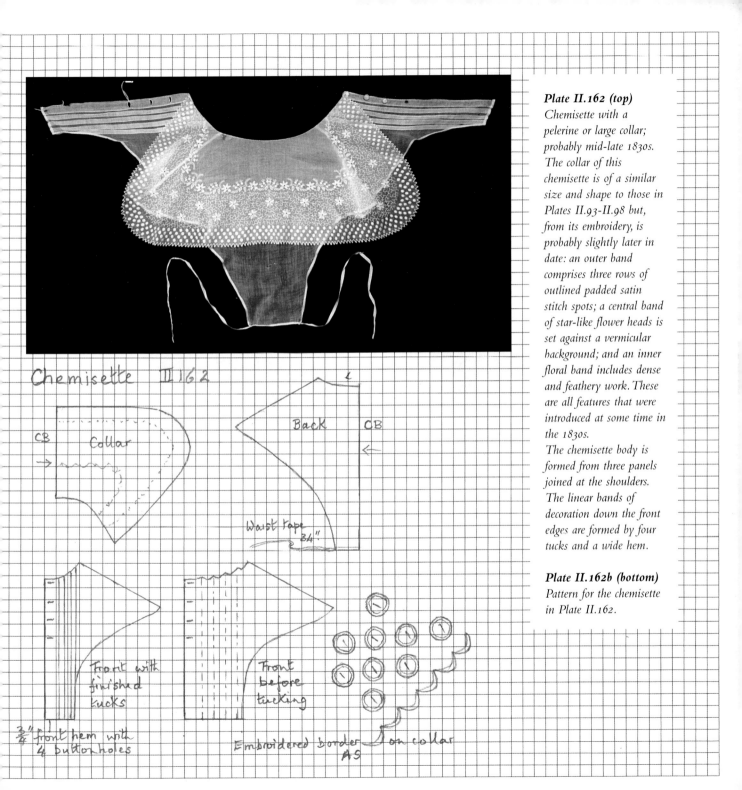

Plate II.162 (top)

Chemisette with a pelerine or large collar; probably mid-late 1830s. The collar of this chemisette is of a similar size and shape to those in Plates II.93-II.98 but, from its embroidery, is probably slightly later in date: an outer band comprises three rows of outlined padded satin stitch spots; a central band of star-like flower heads is set against a vermicular background; and an inner floral band includes dense and feathery work. These are all features that were introduced at some time in the 1830s.

The chemisette body is formed from three panels joined at the shoulders. The linear bands of decoration down the front edges are formed by four tucks and a wide hem.

Plate II.162b (bottom)

Pattern for the chemisette in Plate II.162.

Chemisette II 162

CB Collar

Back CB

Waist tape 34"

Front with finished tucks

Front before tucking

¾" front hem with 4 buttonholes

Embroidered border on collar
AS

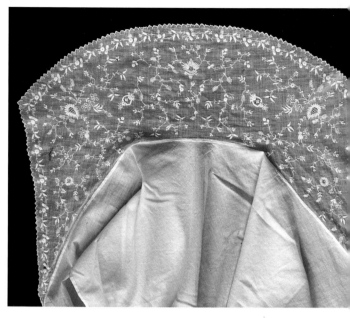

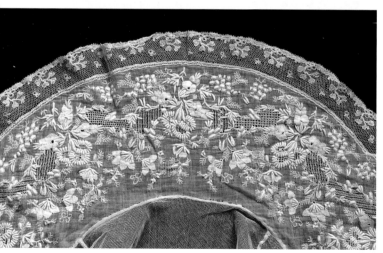

Plate II.163 (top left) *Detail from a portrait of Mrs. Alice Coryndon Rowe (1769-1844): probably late 1830s-early 1840s: Lawrence House Museum, Launceston: Cat. No. LAULH 1981 426. Mrs. Rowe, an ex-Mayoress of Launceston, wears a close-fitting cap and a whiteworked collar with an all-over meandering floral design and gathered frill.*

Plate II.164 (top right) *Whiteworked collar carried by a chemisette: late 1830s-early 1840s: Devonshire Collection. The meandering floral design is fairly similar to that of Mrs. Rowe's collar.*

Plate II.165 (bottom left) *Detail from another whiteworked collar carried by a chemisette: the frill is of bobbin lace: late 1830s-early 1840s: Devonshire Collection. This collar has a very full, elaborate design, worked in a variety of stitches, features gradually becoming more common from the later 1830s.*

Plate II.166 Opposite page) *Patterns for the chemisettes in Plates II.176, II.182, II.188 and II.191.*

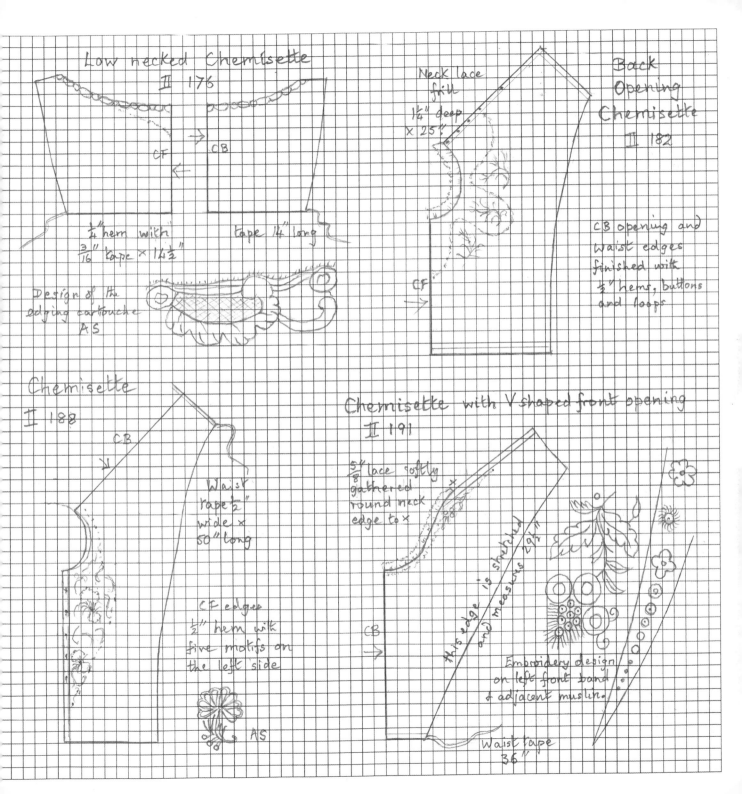

Low necked Chemisette
II 176

CF CB

Design of the
edging cartouche
A5

¼" hem with
3/16" tape × 1½"

tape 14" long

Neck lace
frill
1¼" deep
× 25"

CF

Back
Opening
Chemisette
II 182

CB opening and
waist edges
finished with
½" hems, buttons
and loops

Chemisette
II 188

CB

Waist
tape ½"
wide ×
50" long

CF edges
½" hem with
five motifs on
the left side

A5

Chemisette with V shaped front opening
II 191

5/8" lace softly
gathered
round neck
edge to ×

CB

This edge is stretched
and measures 29½"

Embroidery design
on left front band
& adjacent muslin.

Waist tape
36"

Chemisettes with low-cut necklines or back openings, modesty pieces and a bertha (1820s to 1840s)

Before continuing to follow the development of collars and fichus from the late 1830s into the 1840s, we shall look at alternative versions of the chemisette which were designed specifically for wear with low-cut necklines. These were the general, though not invariable, rule for evening wear and acceptable with some day wear.

The main form of chemisette worn with such necklines had a low neckline complementing that of the bodice with perhaps a frill of fine embroidery or lace that just peeped above the edge of the bodice neckline. Such chemisettes could easily be put on over the head and were usually of very simple construction, sometimes being made from a single panel of fabric but more usually comprising two panels seamed at the shoulders. Some surviving examples have very sloping shoulder seams suggesting a date in the late 1830s–1840s to match the cut of bodices of the period but there appears to be no standardisation in these garments. As very little of such chemisettes shows in wear, their decoration is confined to a narrow band around the neckline with sometimes a small V-shaped panel at the front to fill the V-shaped dip in many bodice necklines of the period.

The simple early 19th century designs were well suited to

Plate II.167 (above) Detail from a fashion illustration of 1827. The two ladies both wear chemisettes beneath their low-cut bodices: that on the left fills the V-shape formed by the cross-over style of bodice while only the dentate upper edge of that on the right is seen above the almost straight neckline. One dress is a day dress while the other is evening wear.

Plate II.168 (right) Detail from a chemisette with a low neckline and sloping shoulders decorated with a simple, repetitive embroidery design and a buttonholed pointed edge. The shoulder line makes this chemisette suitable for wear with the dress of 1841 in Plate II.169 but the embroidery style is much earlier: similar necklines were fashionable from the 1820s to 1840s.
Wneckline - 14½in (37cm);
Dembroidery - ½in (1.3cm)

these narrow bands and continued in use even as the new designs we have already seen were introduced.

At times the chemisette might be replaced by a small piece of fabric that just filled in the V-shaped dip in the neckline. This is what was termed a 'modesty piece' in later periods: I use that term here for the examples in Plates II.178 and 179. At other times a chemisette with a higher neckline, greater depth of decoration and back opening was worn though there appear to be fewer surviving examples of this type: one example is shown in Plate II.182.

Plate II.169 (above) Detail from a fashion illustration of 1841. The lady wears a dress said to be for morning visits: a white chemisette shows just above the low neckline. Either of the chemisettes shown in Plates II.168 and II.170 could be worn with this dress.

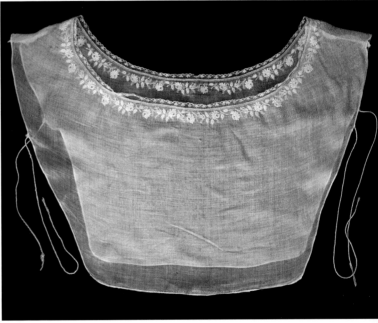

Plate II.170 Chemisette with a low neckline decorated with a narrow band of embroidery and a narrow point-ground bobbin lace frill. The almost continuous band of embroidery is in fact made up of separate rose sprays. The scale and style of the motifs are similar to those of the pattern of 1841 in Plate II.172.

The chemisette is unusual in having ties under the arms to fasten it. The shoulder seams have been altered to give them a greater slope.
D embroidery - 1in (2.5cm): D lace - ¼in (0.7cm)

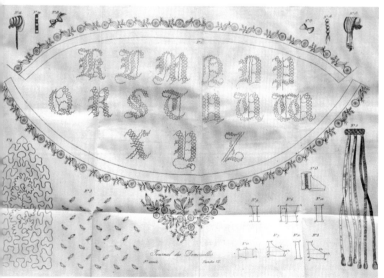

Plate II.171 (top left) *Detail from a fashion illustration of 1835. The neckline of the striped orange-brown evening dress dips markedly at the centre front. The white chemisette worn beneath it is decorated to fill the V-shaped gap as well as to provide an enticing frill round the upper edge. A whitework pattern with a similar embroidery arrangement is shown below.*

Plate II.172 (bottom left) *Embroidery pattern from the Journal des Demoiselles for 1841.*
This page is typical of the period in showing a mix of patterns for embroidery and garments on different scales. Included are patterns for the back and front necklines of a chemisette: these surround the letters of the alphabet. The neckline itself is formed by a simple hem but inside this is a narrow band of discrete floral motifs with an additional V-shaped spray at the front.
Bottom left is a tie end with a vermicular pattern, a common linear design of the period: the spot pattern of tiny leaves to its right could have been used at any time in the first half of the 19th century or even later.

Plate II.173 (opposite top) *Chemisette with a low neckline decorated with a band of embroidery which dips at the front and is bounded by a sinuous laurel trail.*
Most of the embroidery is very simple in character and could have been worked at any time from 1800-1850. Only the floral sprig at centre front suggests a date from the 1820s-mid 1830s for the chemisette: the fillings are of needlepoint lace.
The shoulder seams are piped and, less usually, strengthened with applied panels of fabric for the attachment of shoulder ties. It has the usual waist ties at the back.
CF - 12in (30.5cm); CB - 8³⁄₈in (20.3cm); L shoulder 6¼in (16cm); Wneck - 12½in (32cm); D max embroidery - 4in (10cm)

Plate II.174 (left) *Chemisette with a low neckline decorated with a band of embroidery and a bobbin lace frill: mid 1830s-early 1840s. The floral embroidery forms a V-shape at the centre front and narrows into a band surrounding the neckline which is finished with an unusually open bobbin lace. The chemisette body is unusually short for the 1830s but cannot be of earlier date because of the embroidery. The shoulder seams have been altered. The bottom edges of both front and back panels are formed with casings for draw strings. CB (excluding lace) - 6in (15.2cm); CF (excluding lace) - 5⅛in (13cm); Dmax embroidery - 3¼in (8.2cm); Dmax lace - ⅞in (2.2cm)*

Plate II.174a (right) *Detail of the chemisette in Plate II.174.*

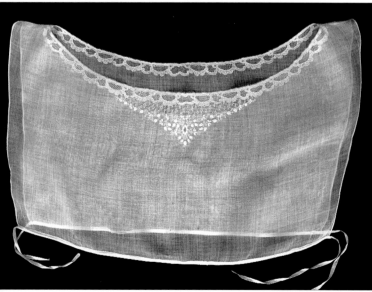

Plate II.175 (above) *Detail of a chemisette with a low neckline: late 1830s-early 1840s: Blaise Castle Cat. No. TA.2837*
The overall style of the chemisette is similar to that shown in Plate II.174 except that the body is longer. Its joy is its embroidered design of, possibly, an Indian drummer kneeling in front of his drum beneath a canopy in a garden. This is worked in a greater variety of stitches than most previous embroideries shown. The design is perhaps rather eccentric for display on a lady's bosom but accords with the desire for novelty in the later 1830s when inspiration was taken from the near and far East as well as earlier centuries.

Plate II.176 (left) *Chemisette with a low neckline: late 1830s-early 1840s. The narrow band of embroidery round the neckline consists of cartouches in appliqué work filled with pulled fillings inspired by 18th-century Dresden work. The neck edge is buttonholed and finished with a bobbin picot edging.*
CB - 9in (23cm); CF - 9in (23cm); W shoulders - 20¾in (63cm); Dmax embroidery - 2¾in (7cm)

Plate II.176a (above left) Detail of the chemisette in Plate II.176. A band of drawn work separates the cartouches from the triangle of embroidery. See p127 for pattern

Plate II.177 (top right) Cuff with a similar combination of embroidery to the chemisette in Plate II.176: late 1830s-1840s. D - 3in (7.6cm); W - 7³⁄₈in (18.8cm)

Plate II.178 (right middle) Modesty piece with a simple dentate upper edge above a wide band of drawn-thread work and a single floral motif: late 1820s-mid 1830s Harris M & AG.

Plate II.179 (right bottom) Modesty piece with two narrow bands of Valenciennes bobbin lace, one along its upper edge, one just beneath it. Almost the entirety of the embroidered space is filled with pulled-thread fillings bounded by C- and S-shaped scrolls: the floral decoration is reduced to tiny leaves and flower heads. This, like the embroidery on the chemisette in Plate II.176, is inspired by Dresden work: more of this work will be seen in other accessories from the late 1830s-early 1840s.
Wmax - 14in (35.5cm); CF (muslin) - 7¼in (18.2cm)
Dmax - embroidery - 1⁷⁄₈in (4.8cm); lace - ³⁄₈in (1cm)

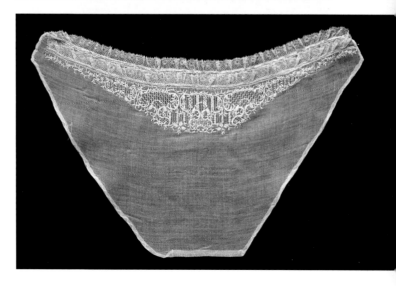

Not all low-cut bodices were worn with chemisettes with almost equally low necklines: back-opening chemisettes with high or half-high necklines were also worn though rather less often to judge by the paucity of surviving examples. The fashion illustrations of 1832 and 1844 (Plates II.180 and II.181) show two examples but earlier and later examples could have been selected. Plates II.182, II.182a show a surviving example.

The fashion illustrations are, in reality, very tiny with sketchy embroidery designs but they clearly show the greater space available for decoration on chemisettes with higher necklines free of deep collars. The surviving example has a deep band of embroidery including floral swags and sprays made up from tiny flower heads and leaves: their character is fairly similar to that of a meandering floral design on a collar pattern shown in Plate II.183. This latter is printed on muslin ready for working, together with the manufacturer's label 'THOS GOULD & CO GLASGOW 1841'.

The chemisette came with a group of whiteworked accessories from the 1830s-1840s, all from one family. It includes a handkerchief with a bobbin lace edging identical to that of the chemisette and with the name 'Annette' embroidered in one corner (Plate II.182b, p136). This is the first handkerchief of the period illustrated: more can be seen on pages 176-185.

Plate II.180 (top left) *Detail from a fashion illustration of 1832: Harris M & AG.*
The lady on the left wears a chemisette with a half-high neckline: two bands of decoration show above her low-cut bodice.

Plate II.181 (bottom left) *Detail from a fashion illustration of 1844. The lady wears a chemisette with bands of decoration extending into the neckline which is finished with a gathered frill. Decorated white sleeves show under her open dress sleeves: these may be part of the chemisette as sleeved chemisettes, though not common, are known from this period.*

Plate II.182 (top left)
Chemisette; probably early
1840s. The chemisette has no
seams. It fastens down the back
with 6 mother-of-pearl buttons and
buttonholed loops. The side edges
are piped, the neck and bottom
edges hemmed, and the back edges
faced. See p127 for pattern

Plate II.182a (bottom left) Detail
of the chemisette in Plate II.182.
The delicate swags and flower sprays
lack the very strong contrast between
dense and feathery motifs seen in many
embroideries of the mid-late 1830s. They
are also very different from neo-classical swags
in late 18th-early 19th century designs. They
do, however, resemble the floral designs in patterns
of 1841 in plates II.183 and II.184. The padded
satin stitch is beautifully graduated to form individual
motifs. The desire for variety is catered for by rather oddly-
placed diamond shapes. Fillings are of pulled-thread work.
The neck frill is of Buckinghamshire point bobbin lace.

Plate II.183 (above) Drawing of a pattern (half shown) for a deep
collar printed on stiffened muslin stamped with the name of the
Glasgow manufacturer 'Thomas Gould & Co' and date '1841':
Glasgow Museums, the Burrell collection, Cat. No. 1926.20. The
pattern is clearly intended to be worked professionally as the stamp
includes the text 'Days allowed to finish this piece': unfortunately it
does not state the number of days allowed.

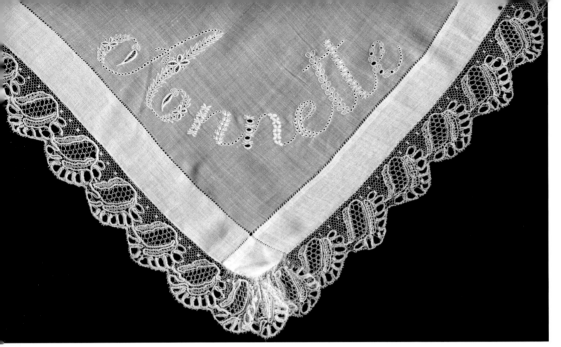

Plate II.182b (top left)
Corner of a handkerchief embroidered with the name 'Annette' from the same family as the chemisette in Plate II.182: the lace is identical to that on the chemisette. The slope and style of the letters, with ornamentation of the upright strokes, is similar to that of letters in a printed pattern of 1841(Plate II.184). The handkerchief is plain apart from the name and border.
30in (76.3cm) x 31½in (80cm) including 1in (2.5cm) hem and 1⅛in (3cm) lace

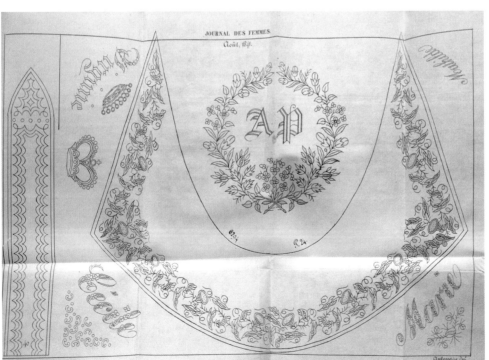

Plate II.184 (bottom left)
Page of patterns from the 'Journal des Femmes' of August 1841. The patterns include the names 'Cecile' and 'Marie' in letters resembling those of 'Annette' in Plate II.182b but also include letters in different styles.

While looking at accessories for low-cut bodices, there is one
further item that can be shown, the bertha collar that often
surrounded evening necklines from the 1830s onwards. Most
of the surviving examples are of lace or embroidered net as
these were more appropriate for evening wear but a pattern
for such a collar in blue ink on muslin can be seen in Plates
II.186, 186a. It is shown with a pattern for a matching
flounce: how these might be worn is shown in Plate II.185.

Plate II.185 (above) Detail from a fashion illustration of 1842
showing evening dress. The lady wears a deep bertha collar round
her low-cut, off-the-shoulder neckline and three tiers of lace flounces
on the skirt.

Plate II.186 (below) Unworked pattern for a bertha collar drawn
in washable blue ink on muslin: late 1830s-early 1840s. The boat-
shaped curvature of the neckline is typical of mid 19th-century
berthas. A fragment from a deep flounce with a pattern repeat
matching that of the bertha is shown beside it: several yards of the
flounce with multiple pattern repeats would be needed to go even
once round the hem of an 1840s evening skirt, never mind three
times as shown in Plate II.185. See next page for detail.
CB - 8½in (21.5cm); D ends - 8in (20.3cm); L neck - 41in (104cm)
Dmax flounce - 13½in (34.5cm); PR - 7½in (19cm)

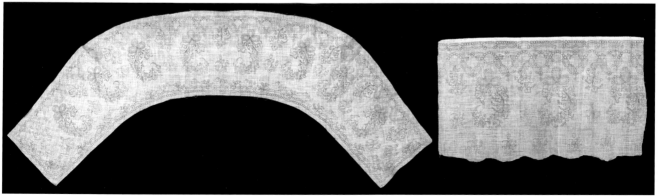

Plate II.186a (above) Detail of the embroidery pattern for the bertha in Plate II.186. The floral design is fairly similar in style to that of the chemisette in Plate II.182 but incorporates spaces for fillings. The main floral spray resembles the boteh designs of cashmere shawls.

THE LATE 1830s TO 1840s
Chemisettes with embroidered fronts or shawl collars

Plate II.182 showed a back-opening chemisette for filling a low-cut bodice with attraction-drawing decoration but, as the V-neckline became more firmly established in the late 1830s and tended to drop in line with the lowering waistline, front-opening chemisettes with decoration down the front panels became more common. These might have a round neckline, as seen in Plate II.188, sometimes finished with a small, neat round collar, or a V-neckline of rather more decorous shape than the bodice (Plate II.191). Alternatively the neckline might be finished with a shawl collar which turns back over the bodice neckline as in Plate II.190. Many necklines were also finished with a lace frill. A few examples of these various forms will be seen in the following pages.

Plate II.187 (bottom left) Detail from a fashion illustration of 1846. The extremely deep V-neckline of one lady's bodice (left) is filled with a front-opening chemisette with embroidery down the front and a frill round the neckline: that on the right is filled with a back-opening chemisette with a small round collar.

Plate II.188 (opposite page, bottom left) Front-opening chemisette: late 1830s-early 1840s. This has a substantial panel of superb embroidery down the front which continues round the back of the high, round neckline. It fastens by means of a tape at the lower back and a single mother-of-pearl button and buttonholed loop at the neck (it may have lost one other button). See p127 for pattern CB - 16in (40.7cm); L front edges - 14¼in (36.2cm); L embroidery down front - 11in (28cm)

138

Plate II.188a (top right) *Detail of the chemisette in Plate II.188. The front edges of the chemisette are hemmed: that seen on the right (left in wear) is also decorated with embroidery and intended to cover the other edge in wear. A line of openwork bordered by one trailed line and one buttonholed line runs inside the hems down the front and round the neck. The dense, quirky design and complexity of the embroidery date this to the late 1830s-early 1840s.*

Plate II.188b (bottom right) *Closer detail of the chemisette in Plate II.188. Flat, dense areas of the design are worked in shadow stitch with embroidered detail over the surface. All but two fillings are pulled work. The padded satin stitch is superbly graduated: all lines are trailed.*

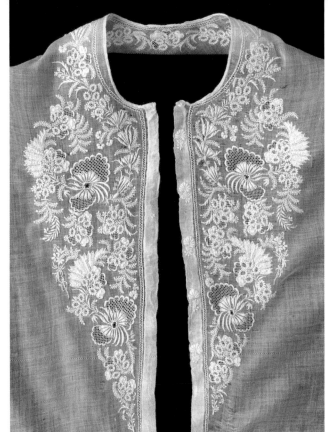

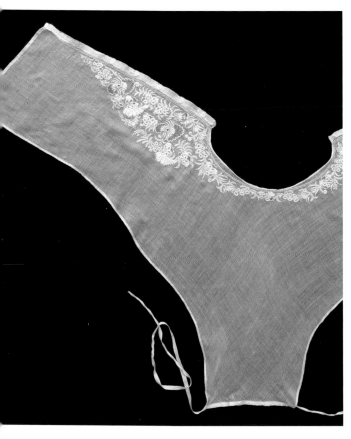

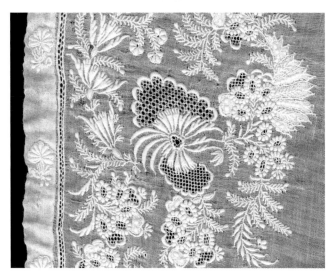

Plate II.189 (left) *Detail from a fashion illustration of the early 1840s. A whiteworked shawl collar borders the low V-neckline of the bodice: it may be carried by a chemisette such as that in Plate II.193: the chemisette in Plate II.190 is better suited to a bodice with a cross-over neckline.*

Plate II.190a (below) *Detail of the shawl collar in Plate II.190. The embroidery is beautifully executed and includes dense feathery scrolls in lightly-padded satin stitch forming cartouches filled with a variety of pulled-thread work in imitation of 18th century Dresden work. All lines are trailed and the outer edge is bordered by a line of openwork between a trailed line and applied thread held with buttonhole stitches. The edges are rolled and trimmed with two different Valenciennes bobbin laces: a lace trimming inside the neck edge of such chemisettes is quite usual.*

Plate II.190 (below) *Chemisette with a very open V-neckline and shawl collar: late 1830s–early 1840s. The body comprises a single panel of fabric without shoulder seams but naturally takes up the sloping shoulder line typical of the late 1830s–40s in wear.*

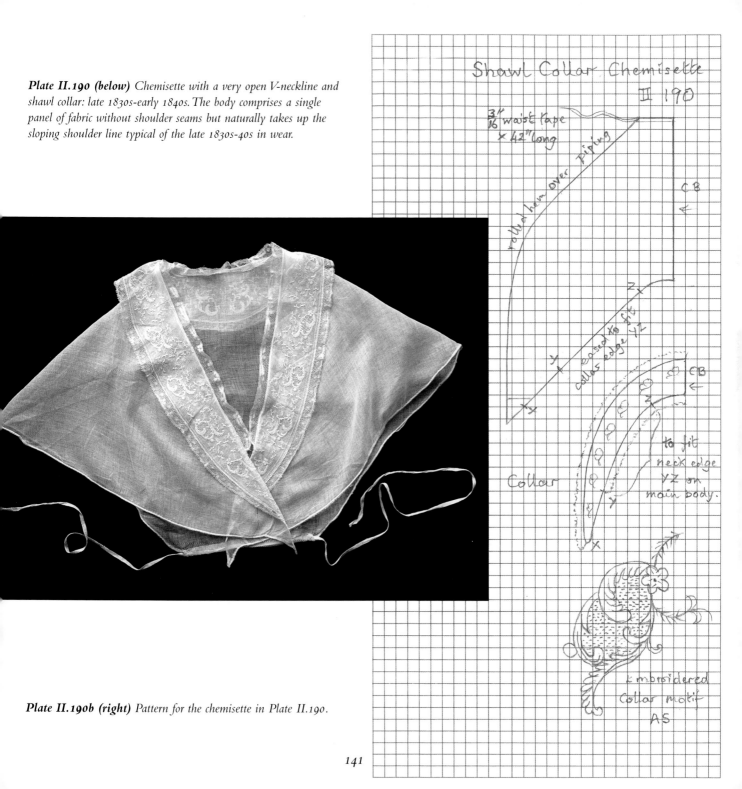

Shawl Collar Chemisette
II 190

3/16" waist tape × 42" long

rolled hem over Piping

CB

Z

eased to fit

collar edge YZ

CB

to fit
neck edge
YZ on
main body.

Collar

Embroidered
Collar motif
AS

Plate II.190b (right) *Pattern for the chemisette in Plate II.190.*

141

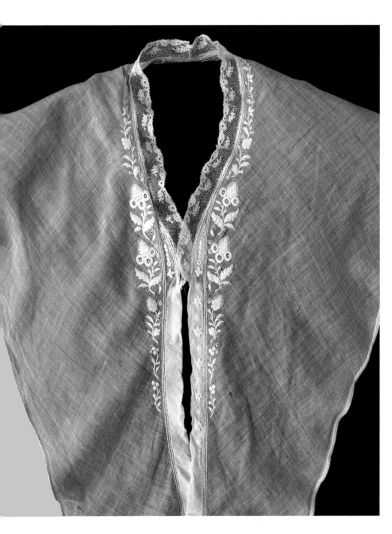

Plate II.191a (left) Closer detail of the chemisette in Plate II.191.

This has a much more modest, more usual band of embroidery round the neck than that in Plate II.188 but it is just as beautifully worked. A line of openwork with trailed lines each side runs inside the front hems and round the neck. Dense pattern areas are in padded satin stitch and very close dots created by chain stitch on the reverse. Needlepoint lace stitches fill the larger eyelets which are surrounded by padded satin stitch and trailed rings.

Plate II.191 (above) Detail of a chemisette with a V-shaped front opening: late 1830s-1840s. This is cut from a single panel of muslin with the back on the straight.

The left-hand front hem is embroidered: the neck is trimmed with Buckinghamshire point bobbin lace.

CB - 15in including ¾in lace (38cm inc. 2cm lace)

L lace at neck - 19½in (49.5cm)

See Plate II.166, p127 for pattern

Plate II.192 (opposite top) Detail from a page of patterns published in the 'Journal des Demoiselles' for November 1840.

The description suggests that anyone who does not know how to work the fillings indicated can insert net in their place. The pattern, drawn on fine muslin, could be bought for 2 francs 25c. or '2fr 75 échantillonné, à la brodeuse' (with a sample worked by an embroideress).

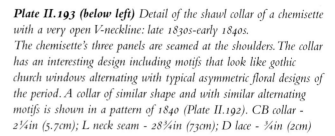

Plate II.193 (below left) *Detail of the shawl collar of a chemisette with a very open V-neckline: late 1830s-early 1840s.*
The chemisette's three panels are seamed at the shoulders. The collar has an interesting design including motifs that look like gothic church windows alternating with typical asymmetric floral designs of the period. A collar of similar shape and with similar alternating motifs is shown in a pattern of 1840 (Plate II.192). CB collar - 2¼in (5.7cm); L neck seam - 28¾in (73cm); D lace - ¾in (2cm)

Plate II.193a (below right) *Detail of the collar in Plate II.193.*
The surprising 'church window' design, in the Gothic taste, is in fact typical of the search for novelty in design in the late 1830s-1840s. The Valenciennes bobbin lace trimming the neck edge is sewn to a piped seam. The outer edge of the collar is finished with a ⅛in (0.3cm) openwork band between a trailed line and a buttonholed edge with a minute bobbin-picot trimming.

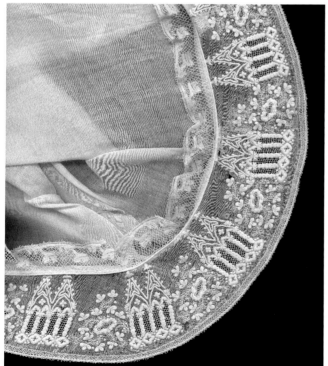

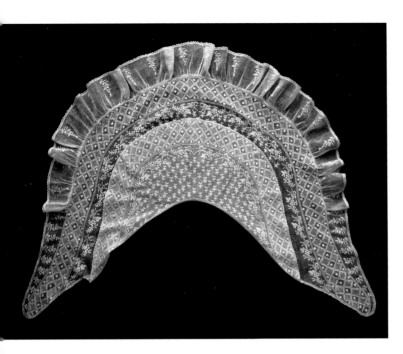

A few more fichus and a cuff

Before turning to chemisettes for bodices with low necklines, we saw various accessories from the second half of the 1830s. At this time pelerines were still quite wide, with sharp or rounded points spreading onto the shoulders. Their necklines, however, were often smoothly curved so that they naturally formed a V-shape similar to the necklines just seen.

By the late 1830s dress sleeves had tightened over the shoulders, the waistline had dropped, often to a V-shape at the front, and skirts had widened yet further. These changes had a very marked effect on a lady's silhouette: the exuberant hour-glass shape of 1825-35 created by the high, wide shoulder line, narrow waist and full skirt, gave way to a more demure, conical outline, a style that demanded new forms of accessory.

We have already seen the new forms of chemisettes which filled the V-necklines of this style but the outer accessories, the pelerines, or fichus as they were often called by then, also changed. They gradually lost the bulbous curves or sharp points that had given them their width over the shoulders: their smooth outer edges became more often trimmed with a gathered lace or whitework frill and extended into long pointed lappets at the front. This new style could wrap closely around the body, continuing the conical line of the shoulders into the skirts while the long pointed ends complemented the V-shaping of the new waistline. Capes, mantles and shawls that could wrap around the body likewise became more common, the various forms merging into each other. The story of these outer garments is continued here from the late 1830s.

Plate II.194 (above) Double fichu; late 1830s-early 1840s.
This accessory is very similar in shape and size to that in Plate II.141 and is only slightly less wide but a pattern of 1840 in Plate II.202 shows that fichus with similar outlines were still in use at the end of the 1830s. It is the complexity and banded nature of the pattern, seen for example in the fashion illustration of 1839 in Plate II.196, that suggest that this dates from the very late 1830s-early 1840s. There is also greater use of pulled-thread work than in earlier years. Individual features of the design - the diaper pattern, the spot pattern on the upper layer, the band of discrete sprigs forming almost continuous decoration and the elongate sprigs spreading in from the edges of the gathered frill - are all seen in earlier embroideries showing the difficulty of dating such accessories.
Top layer CB - 7in (17.7cm); neck - 27in (68.5cm); diaper band including borders - 2in (5cm). Bottom layer CB - 11in + 3in frill (28cm + 7.6cm); neck 42in (106.7cm)

Plate II.194a (opposite top left) Detail of the lower layer of the fichu in Plate II.194. Alternate diamonds of the diaper pattern are filled with pulled-thread work and tiny flower heads. The outer, slightly pointed edge of the frill is bordered by a line of openwork between trailed lines, as are the diaper bands. The frill sprigs are long and widely spaced on its wider part but reduce in length and spacing as the frill narrows towards the ends.

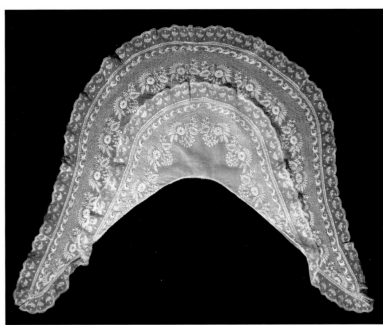

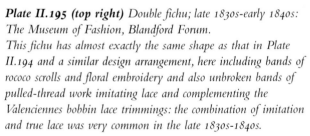

Plate II.195 (top right) *Double fichu; late 1830s-early 1840s: The Museum of Fashion, Blandford Forum.*
This fichu has almost exactly the same shape as that in Plate II.194 and a similar design arrangement, here including bands of rococo scrolls and floral embroidery and also unbroken bands of pulled-thread work imitating lace and complementing the Valenciennes bobbin lace trimmings: the combination of imitation and true lace was very common in the late 1830s-1840s.

Plate II.195a (bottom right) *A detail of the fichu in Plate II.195. The narrow scroll design inside the lace edges is very similar in character to a design of 1841 seen in Plate II.249, p180.*

145

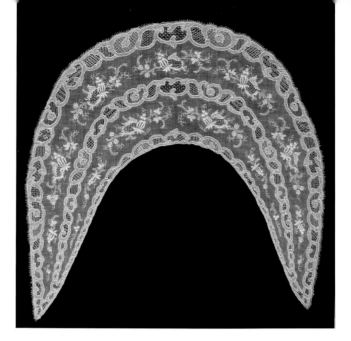

Plate II.196 (top left) *Fashion illustration of October 1839 showing a lady wearing a canezou with banded decoration: it covers the new shoulder line but defines quite a deep V-neckline and comes to a point just below the natural waistline, matching the dip in the bodice waistline. It may be of lace or whitework: lace was becoming more popular and gradually came to oust whitework from its prime position for such accessories.*

Plate II.197 (top right) *Fichu: late 1830s-early 1840s. This fichu has smoothly curved edges that meet at points at the front. Its bands of rococo decoration imitating lace and Dresden whitework look very like the banding on the canezou in Plate II.196. See p119 for pattern*
CB - 5¾in (14.5cm); Wmax - 14¼in (36cm)

Plate II.197a (bottom left) *Detail of the fichu in Plate II.197. The cartouches are formed by appliqué work with fillings of pulled-thread work. The discrete floral motifs between the cartouches are in dense padded satin stitch with feathery leaves like other embroideries of the period but also define open shapes for fillings. The edge is buttonholed and finished with a tiny trimming of bobbin-made picots. The outer border looks very similar to that of Anne Marie Bowden's collar in Plate II.198.*

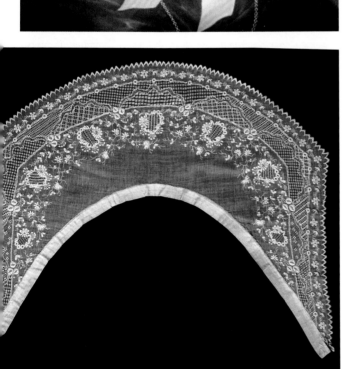

Plate II.198 Detail from a portrait of Anne Marie Bowden, c1840. The lady's cap, with its double frill, probably matches her double collar fastened close around her neck. The cartouches of fancy fillings around the edges look like lace and were popular in lace designs of the period. They were also imitated in whitework as illustrated by the fichu in Plate II.197: both crafts were influenced by 18th-century lace and whitework designs.

Plate II.199 (bottom left)
Collar or fichu: late 1830s-early 1840s. This shows another banded design: simple repetitive floral motifs form an outer border; the next band is almost completely filled with pulled-thread work imitating 18th-century Dresden work; the inner floral border is influenced by the rococo style but is treated very differently from 18th-century work. See Plates I.15, 15a for details and Plate I.14 for Dresden work (p14, 15).

Plate II.200 (right) Cuff: late 1830s-early 1840s.
The central band of delicate floral embroidery is sandwiched between two ¼in-wide bands of pulled-thread work and a narrow Valenciennes bobbin lace whipped on to a buttonholed edge. The cuff fastens around the wrist by means of two mother-of-pearl buttons and corresponding buttonholed loops. Muslin L - 7¾in (19.6cm); W - 1⅝in (4.8cm) W lace - ½in (1.2cm)

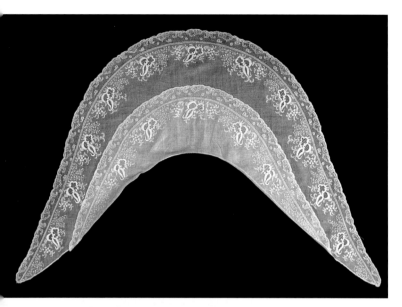

Plate II.201 (left) *Double fichu; late 1830s-early 1840s.*
This shows another design inspired by both Dresden work and lace.
Each panel has a narrow lace-like border of pulled-thread work
incorporating cartouches left in plain fabric with trailed outlines and
eyelet holes for details. A narrow openwork band between trailed
lines separates each border from its main panel just as whiteworked
items are often finished before the addition of a lace trimming.
Main panel: CB - 11in (28cm); Wmax (tip to tip when flat) - 34in
(86.5cm): L neck edge - 40in (101.5cm)
Collar: CB - 6in (15.3cm); Wmax (tip to tip when flat) - 22¾in
(58cm): L neck edge - 29in (73.7cm)
D lace-like border - CB - 1¼in (3.2cm); ends ⅝in (1.6cm)

Plate II.201a (below) *A detail of the fichu in Plate II.201*
showing the lace-like border and an inner rococo border of discrete
motifs including bold curvilinear shapes which provide further space
for fillings combined with delicate floral sprays and coiling tendrils.
The outer edge is trimmed with an edging of machine-made picots.

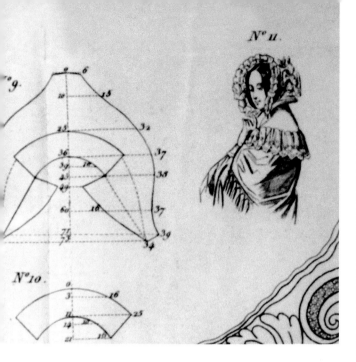

Plate II.202 (above) *Detail from a page of patterns from the 'Journal des Demoiselles' for May 1840 showing a pattern for a collared fichu. The neckline shows the position in which a collar (drawn separately beneath the fichu) should be attached. It also shows cut and fold lines for revers that would fold back over the main panel at the front - a fichu constructed in this manner is shown in Plate II.203. To the right is a lady with a fichu wrapped round her shoulders.*

Plate II.203 (top right) *Collared fichu; late 1830s-early 1840s; Moravian Settlement, Fulneck, Leeds.*
This fichu is constructed in the manner indicated in the pattern of 1840 in Plate II.202: the revers are cut in one piece with the main panel while the collar is cut separately and seamed to the neck edge and ends of the revers which are turned back. The embroidery on the revers is worked on the opposite side of the fabric from that on the main panel so that the right side is uppermost in wear.

Plate II.203a (bottom right) *A detail of the collared fichu in Plate II.203 showing the insertion of the collar in the main panel. The floral motifs lack the filling stitches seen in the last few illustrations but the fichu is of similar date.*

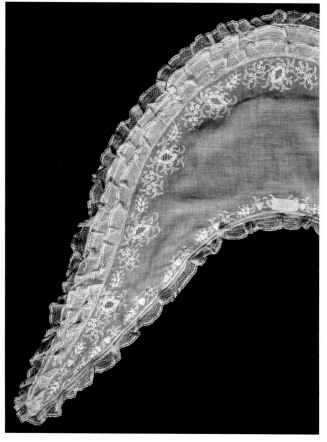

Plate II.204 (top left) *Detail from a fashion illustration of 1839 showing ladies wearing whiteworked fichus drawn close around their shoulders and crossed at the front.*

Plate II.205 (bottom left) *Fichu with lace frills (half shown): late 1830s-early 1840s*
Although this fichu does not have the all-over patterns of the fichus in Plate II.204, it would have looked very like the left-hand fichu in wear. It is bordered by bands of rococo floral decoration and gathered frills of machine lace, three round its outer edge and one along the neck edge. Fully-patterned machine laces were available from 1841: simple designs like this could be worked in the 1830s.

Plate II.205a (above right) *Detail of the fichu in Plate II.205*

Plate II.206 (above left) *Detail from a fashion illustration from the magazine 'London and Paris': late 1830s. This shows two variations on the fichu theme of the period: that on the left is perhaps best termed a shawl or mantle. It has a deep whiteworked frill and long ends which cascade down the front of the skirt.*

Plate II.207 (top right) *Fichu with lace frills: late 1830s-early 1840s This is rather smaller than the mantle in Plate II.206 but has a very similar embroidered border and a wide, gathered frill along its outer edge though here it is of lace rather than whitework: a narrower frill finishes the neck edge.*
D lace - narrow - ¾in (2cm); wider - 3in (7.6cm)

Plate II.207a (bottom right) *A detail of the fichu in Plate II.207. Both frills are of Buckinghamshire point bobbin lace: they are sewn to the underside of the fichu alongside a narrow openwork and trailed band inside the neatly scalloped edge.*

A variety of capes, canezous and other accessories

It is impossible to deal with the multitude of different, or slightly different, whiteworked accessories in use in the 1830s-40s in a purely chronological order: all were worn simultaneously over a number of years; one form merged into another; all might have round or V necklines, with or without collars; and the embroidery styles varied considerably as already seen. The next group of accessories will demonstrate the problem.

Plate II.209 (opposite top left) Fichu-canezou: late 1830s-1840s This accessory has almost exactly the same shape as that in Plate II.208, even to the curves of its outer edges which are convex over the shoulders, changing to concave down the front. Only the neckline, with its neat round collar, differs. The back is shorter than the front, matching the bodice waistline of the period which usually ends in a point below the natural waistline at the front but is straight and slightly higher at the back. The lower back is embroidered all round but gathered to a 1½in long, ½in wide piece of tape on the inside. It also has an all-over design but this is very different from that in the fashion illustration: it is tamboured and therefore linear in character.

1840S DICKENS' NOVELS; BERLIN WOOL-WORK BECAME POPULAR AS A FORM OF AMATEUR EMBROIDERY

1840 PENNY POST INTRODUCED

1841 QUEEN VICTORIA AND PRINCE ALBERT MARRIED AND HAD SEVEN CHILDREN BY 1850; APPLICATION OF THE JACQUARD DEVICE TO LACE-MAKING MACHINES ENABLED FULLY-PATTERNED LACE TO BE MADE

1842 VERDI'S 'NABUCCO'

1843 PUNCH PUBLISHED THOMAS HOOD'S 'THE SONG OF THE SHIRT' DECRYING THE POOR WAGES OF SEAMSTRESSES; EDWARD LEAR'S 'BOOK OF NONSENSE' PUBLISHED; WORDSWORTH MADE POET LAUREATE

1844 TURNER'S 'RAIN, STEAM AND SPEED – THE GREAT WESTERN RAILWAY'

1846 ELECTRIC TELEGRAPH CO. FORMED

Plate II.208 (above) Detail from a fashion illustration of 1838-39 showing a lady wearing what may have been called a fichu-canezou. This fits fairly closely round the neck with slight V shaping, extends just onto the shoulders and narrows at the front to finish below the natural waistline in straight ends. It is decorated with an all-over floral pattern in the rococo style.

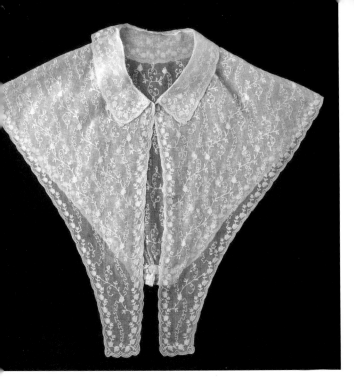

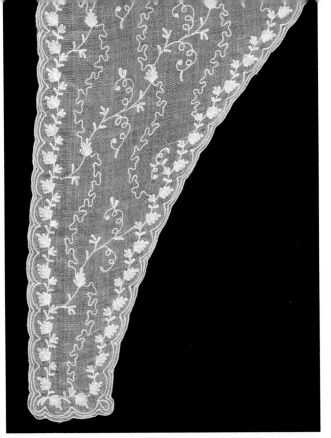

Plate II.209a (above right)
Detail of the fichu-canezou in Plate II.209. The design is an interesting combination of serpentine wiggly lines crossed by sinuous stems carrying leaves and coiling tendrils. Both of these motifs might be seen in late-18th century embroideries but not normally in combination. The outer edges are very slightly scalloped, rolled and buttonholed outside two scalloped tamboured lines and a trailing leafy stem. CB - 15in (38cm); L front edges - 15½in (39.5cm); W shoulders - 19¾in (50cm); L shoulder seam - 9in (23cm); D collar - 2in (5cm); L neck seam - 15¾in (34cm)

Plate II.209b (below) *Detail of the collar of the fichu-canezou in Plate II.209.*

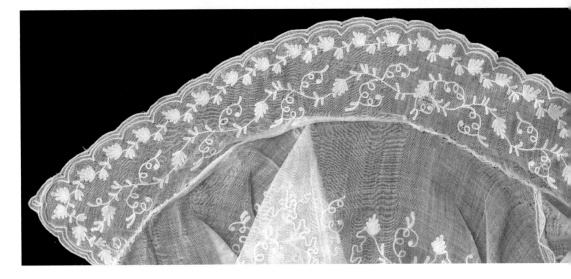

Plate II.210 (right) *Drawing of a fichu-canezou: probably late 1830s: St.Fagans, Cat. No. 62.52.30*
This accessory is again similar in shape to those in Plates II.208 and II.209 apart from the unusual embroidered collar detail which extends the shoulder line slightly. This suggests that it dates from the mid 1830s when the dress shoulder line was wider but the elongate triangular floral decoration suggests a late 1830s-early 1840s date - see Plates II.146, 147.

Plate II.210a (below) *Detail of the back of the fichu-canezou in Plate II.210.*

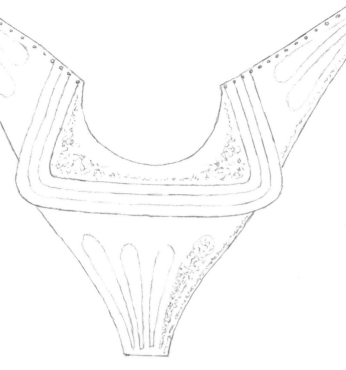

Plate II.210b (below) *Detail of a shoulder and upper back of the fichu-canezou in Plate II.210. The four parallel lines apparently delineating a collar are embroidered on the single panel constituting the canezou.*

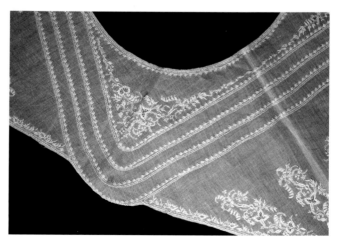

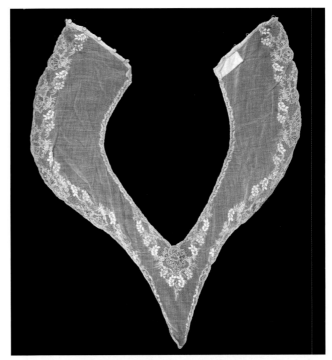

Plate II.211 (above) *Detail from a fashion illustration of 1842 showing a lady in evening dress. The lady's bodice is decorated with a plastron (a decorative panel covering a bodice front) which extends to a point at the dipped waistline and into a collar which surrounds the low neckline. She also wears a short cape. Both accessories are probably of lace but could be of whitework as demonstrated by the examples which follow.*

Plate II.212 (top right) *Plastron and collar: late 1830s–early 1840s: Blaise Castle Cat. No. TA 1880.*
The general shape and embroidery style of this back-opening accessory proclaim it to be of similar date to the fichu-canezous in preceding Plates: it resembles one accessory shown in the fashion illustration of 1842 in Plate II.211.

Plate II.212a (bottom right) *Detail of the plastron in Plate II.212.*

155

Plate II.214 (below) Fichu-canezou: late 1830s-1840s
This accessory has a collar and revers like those of the accessory in Plate II.213 but the shoulder width of those in Plates II.208-210. The revers are cut in one piece with the main panel: the collar is separate. See Plate II.214c for pattern

Plate II.214a (opposite top left) Detail of the fichu-canezou in Plate II.214 showing the rococo design which, like several others seen previously, is derived from Dresden work.
All edges are trimmed with a narrow bobbin lace.

Plate II.214b (opposite bottom left) A closer detail of the embroidery of the fichu-canezou in Plate II.214.

Plate II.213 (above) Fashion illustration of 1845 showing a lady wearing a fichu or fichu-canezou with a collar and revers. Although having considerable depth at the sides, it is shaped to draw tightly over the shoulders. The panel filling the open front may be part of the accessory or of the underlying bodice.

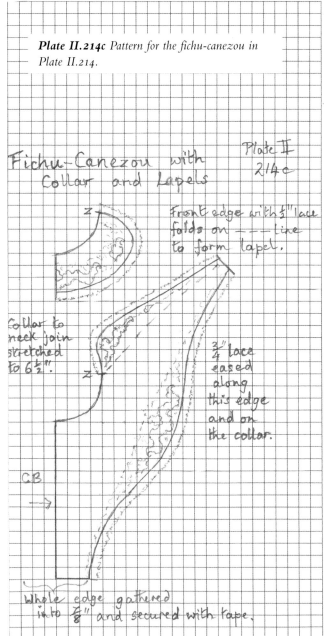

Plate II.214c Pattern for the fichu-canezou in Plate II.214.

Fichu-Canezou with Collar and Lapels

Plate II 214c

z

Front edge with ⅜" lace folds on ---- line to form lapel.

Collar to neck join stretched to 6½".

z

¾" lace eased along this edge and on the collar.

CB
→

Whole edge gathered into ⅞" and secured with tape.

157

Plate II.215 (left) *Detail from a fashion illustration of 1842 showing a lady wearing a collared cape, or 'canezou' according to the new usage of the word in Plate II.218. The narrow shoulder line of the late 1830s-1840s lent itself to the wearing of capes: their line continued into the skirts, giving the whole outfit a roughly conical shape. Both short capes like that shown here and long capes or mantles, which will be seen later, were popular.*

Plate II.216 (below left) *Collared cape (half shown): late 1830s-1840s; Worthing Museum Cat. No. 1965.777*
This is of very similar style and shape to that shown in Plate II.215, even to the arrangement of the decoration which includes distinct outer and inner bands of embroidery although here the latter consists solely of a narrow border rather than the all-over decoration in the fashion illustration.
The design includes a fascinating mixture of motifs - rococo scrolls; shell and star-like features; twiggy branches and leafy scrolls - together with rectangular insertions of machine lace inside a tiny dentate buttonholed edge.
CF - 8½in (21.5cm); CB - 12¾in (32cm); CF collar - 6½in (16.5cm); CB - 4¾in (12cm)

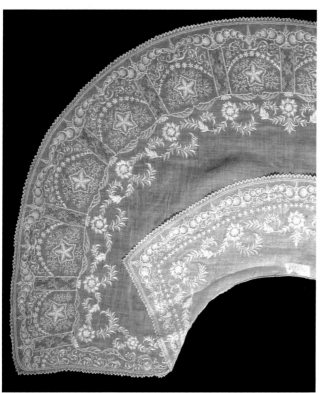

Plate II.216a (above) *Detail of the collared cape in Plate II.216.*

Plate II.217 (above) *Page of patterns from the 'Journal des Demoiselles' of December 1841: bottom right - rich handkerchief corner; left centre - collar for tambouring or chain stitch; bottom left - cuff; centre - bag - vermicular lines were popular for filling large areas of ground as they had been in the early-mid 18th century.*

Plate II.218 (right) *Detail from a fashion illustration from the periodical 'London and Paris' of 1847 showing three different styles of accessory all of which are termed 'canezous' although we might now term them 'capes'.*

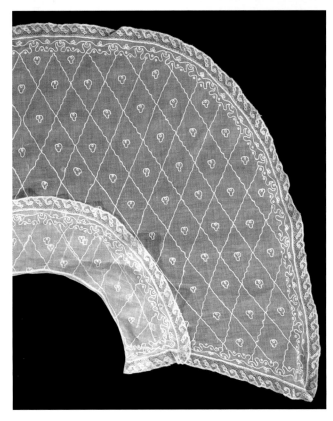

Plate II.219 (top left) *Collared cape, or canezou: late 1830s-40s. A simply-shaped cape has already been seen in Plate II.216. This example is smaller, but of similar cut: the single, approximately semi-circular panel in fine muslin shapes naturally to a sloping shoulder-line with its edges meeting at the front. The main difference lies in its tamboured decoration but the slightly wavy diaper pattern with a motif within each diamond is similar to that of the collar pattern of 1841 in Plate II.217.*
CB - 12¾in (32.3cm); L front edge - 11½in (29.2cm); L neck seam - 18½in (47cm), all including ⅝in (1.2cm) lace.

Plate II.219a (bottom left) *Detail showing half the collared cape in Plate II.219 laid flat.*

Plate II.219b (top right) *Detail of the collared cape in Plate II.219. The scrolling, vermicular and wavy tamboured lines are similar to those in the patterns of 1841 in Plate II.217.*
The machine-lace trimming has a design outlined with a thick thread run in by hand in imitation of the gimp thread outlining patterns in bobbin lace: in the 1840s machines were not yet able to introduce a thicker thread.

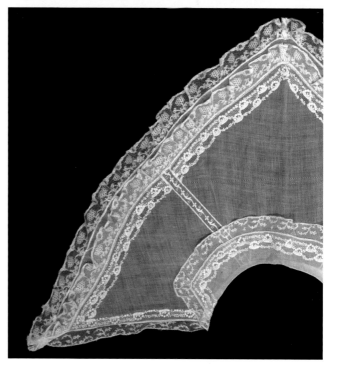

Plate II.220 (above) *Fashion illustration of 1842 showing a lady wearing a cape with a deep collar and revers.*

Plate II.221 (top right) *Collared cape or canezou: late 1830s-40s. Unlike the capes in Plates II.216 and II.219, which are cut in one piece, this has three main panels joined at the shoulders by decorative insertions. Shoulder seams were common in many accessories of the period as they enabled them to sit neatly on the fashionable sloping shoulder line. The embroidery design is very simple but lace frills add extra decoration. These are in two different designs of hand-run machine-made copies of Buckinghamshire point. See Plate II.221c for pattern.*

Plate II.221a (bottom right) *Detail of the cape in Plate II.221.*

Plate II.221b (left)
*Closer detail of the cape in
Plate II.221.
The dense pattern is in padded
satin stitch and shadow work
with additional dots over the
shadow work.*

Plate II.221c (below) *Pattern
for the cape in Plate II.221.*

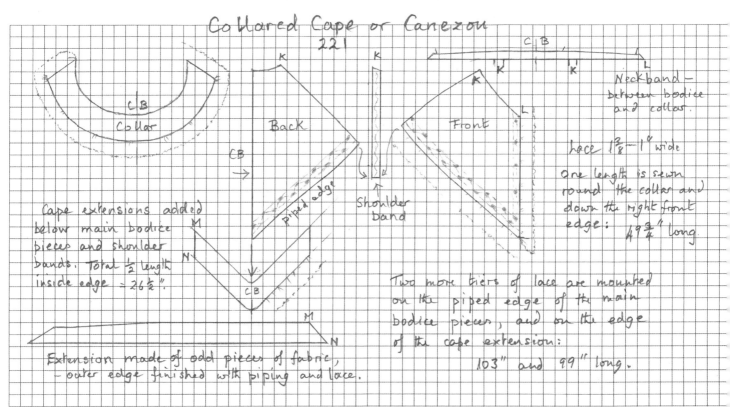

Collared Cape or Canezou
221

Collar
CB
Back
CB
Front
Piped edge
Shoulder Band
CB
M
N
CB
M
N

K K K K K K
CB
L L
L

Neckband –
between bodice
and collar.

Lace 1⅜ – 1" wide

One length is sewn
round the collar and
down the right front
edge: 49¾" long.

Cape extensions added
below main bodice
pieces and shoulder
bands. Total ½ length
inside edge = 26½".

Extension made of odd pieces of fabric,
– outer edge finished with piping and lace.

Two more tiers of lace are mounted
on the piped edge of the main
bodice pieces, and on the edge
of the cape extension:
103" and 99" long.

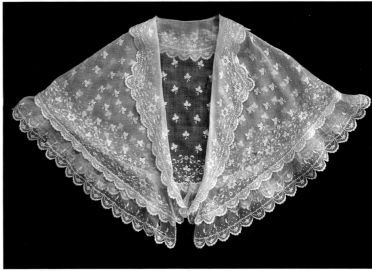

Plate II.222 (top left) Fashion illustration of 1842. The lady, left, wears a cape or fichu with a V-neckline and a shawl collar. It is wrapped tightly around her shoulders and is fastened at the front so that its long pointed ends form hanging lappets. Its gathered, whiteworked edge frill is probably intended to be sewn beneath the main edge like that of the cape in Plate II.223.

Plate II.223 (top right) Collared cape or canezou: 1840s. This, like the cape in Plate II.221, has three main panels with shoulder seams. Its collar extends down its very open V neckline. A continuous, slightly gathered frill, of whitework rather than lace, is sewn beneath the scalloped edges of the main panels. CB - 13¼in (34.6cm); L shoulder seam - 11½in (29.2cm) Collar CB - 3in (7.6cm); Lneck edge - 37¾in (96cm): D frill - 2¾in (7cm)

Plate II.223a (bottom left) Detail of the collared cape in Plate II.223. The embroidery is entirely in heavily padded satin stitch and trailing but for needlepoint lace centres in larger flowers. The border design is based on a fine diaper pattern; the main panels are sprigged except beneath the collar. The fine scalloping of the edges gives a very neat finish.

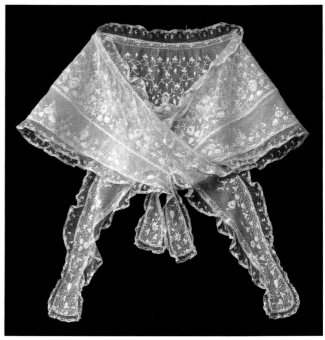

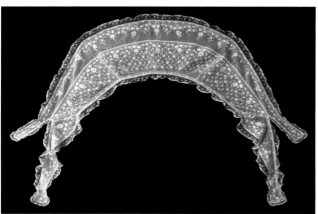

Plate II.224 (above left) *Fashion illustration of 1847 showing a lady wearing a collared cape in many ways similar to that of 1842 in Plate II.222 but its edges are more deeply scalloped, a feature that returned to fashion after the almost smooth edges popular in the late 1830s-mid 1840s.*

Plate II.225 (above right) *A complex fichu: 1840s*
This has a most curious structure: the main body consists of three central panels joined at shoulder seams and an outer panel seamed to the outer edges of the main panels. The outer panel extends into narrow square - ended lappets while wider lappets are added to the ends of the central panels. All the edges are trimmed with Buckinghamshire point bobbin lace.
The diaper pattern of the main panels is very similar to that of the cape in Plate II.223 but the embroidery is more complex.
See Plate I.37 for a detail of the main back panel.

Plate II.225a (left) *The fichu in Plate II.225 laid flat.*

164

Plate II.225b (left) *Detail of the shoulder seam and embroidery of the fichu in Plate II.225.*
The work is almost entirely in dense stitching: the light background of earlier embroideries has entirely disappeared. Shoulder seams are worked in ladder stitch, as are the edges before the addition of the lace frills. Small fillings are pulled, larger areas are seeded by means of chain stitch worked on the back.

The preceding pages have covered most of the major whiteworked accessories of the first half of the 19th century but there were many less important items. There is no room here for them all nor, indeed, for one item that originated in the 1840s but became extremely important in the second half of the century, that is, the white undersleeve, or engageant, that covered the wrist as sleeves shortened. That must await our next book on whiteworked accessories. Here there is just room for a couple of variously-named lappets, ties or cravats before we conclude with a few shawls and mantles and the handkerchiefs that assumed great significance in the late 1830s-1840s.

Plate II.226 (above) *Fashion illustration of 1835 showing a lady wearing a pair of lappets or streamers from her cap.*

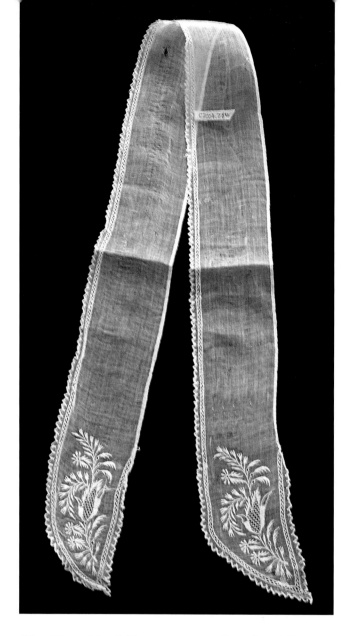

Plate II.228 (below) Detail of one end of a tie or pair of lappets: probably 1840s. This is one end of a long tie like that in Plate II.227 but, being patterned down both edges, might have been worn from the hair or round the neck.

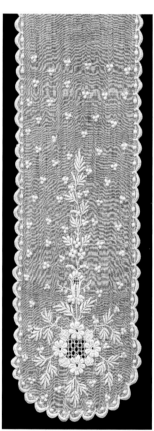

Shawls and mantles (1830s to 1840s)

In our discussion of accessories from the 1820s–1840s we have lost sight completely of the long shawls that helped to create the fashionable look of the early 19th century. Throughout the second quarter of the century long shawls continued to be worn but it was cashmere and other coloured versions that were the rage. Lace versions might be worn with evening wear, either draped round the shoulders or from the hair, but whitework does not appear to have been popular from the paucity of surviving examples.

Naturally the occasional exception can be found that clearly dates from this period but it is only in the later 1830s that whitework shawls appear to have returned to favour, and then in square or triangular form that could wrap closely round the body. The following pages will show just a few examples.

Plate II.227 (above) Tie or cravat: 1830s: Hampshire Collection: Cat. No. C2004.264. This example was probably intended to be worn round the neck as it has one straight edge and one patterned edge. Its bold sprig motif suggests a date in the early-mid 1830s. L - 24in (60cm); W - 2¼in (5.6cm)

Plate II.230a (opposite bottom left) Detail of the embroidery of the long shawl in Plate II.230.

Plate II.230 (left) *One end of a tamboured long shawl: probably 1830s.*

Tambouring, although not popular in the first quarter of the 19th century, came back into use in the later 1830s as seen in several capes and canezous already illustrated. It was particularly useful for large articles such as this shawl as it enabled larger designs to be created more quickly than with a needle. This example has a running floral pattern resembling the design on the lady's skirt of 1836 in Plate II.231. The border also has similarities to the apron borders in Plates II.52, II.54.

Plate II.229 (top right)
Detail from a fashion illustration showing evening dress of 1835. The lady wears a long white shawl with her evening dress: this is probably intended to be of lace but the diaphanous muslin shawl in Plate II.230 is of a similar size and could have been a suitable substitute.

Plate II.231 (bottom right)
Detail from a fashion illustration of 1836 showing a lady with a floral design trailing down her skirt. The linear nature of the design suggests it is tamboured.

Plate II.233 (right) Long shawl or scarf: late 1830s-mid 1840s. This example is much smaller than long shawls seen so far and is probably better termed a 'scarf'.

It also has a wider, more definitely triangular form of floral design than other articles in this work: this form seems to have been more common on square-ended accessories, particularly lace veils and shawls, and on the front panels of ladies' skirts.

L - 89in (226cm);
W - 12in (30.5cm)
D triangular design - 11in (28cm)

Plate II.232 (above) Detail from a fashion illustration of 1839 from 'The Ladies Cabinet' showing dinner dress.

Despite the fact that ladies are supposed to have looked more demure in the late 1830s, the lady in this illustration is clearly enjoying showing off her shawl.

Plate II.233a (left) Detail of the embroidery of the shawl in Plate II.233. The dense motifs are in appliqué work and padded satin stitch. Small fillings are of needlepoint lace, larger ones of pulled-thread work.

Plate II.235 (below) *Detail from a fashion illustration of 1847. Long white shawls continued in fashion illustrations right through the 1840s though designs are usually too small to see.*

Plate II.234 (above) *One end of a tamboured long shawl: probably 1840s. The design of this shawl, though based on a triangle, is far more sprawling than that of the shawl in Plate II.233. It is also far more idiosyncratic in its incorporation of arabesque shapes derived from Middle-Eastern art.*

The next few shawls are of the triangular shape that was popular from the 1830s. These are often larger than the 18th-century kerchiefs, even the buffons from the end of the century, and were worn round the shoulders with the main point draped onto the back of the skirt. Like their early 19th-century predecessors they are usually decorated along all three edges: their main decorative features naturally accord with those of other 19th-century accessories. In fine muslin, they provided a light, summer alternative to the cashmere or woollen shawls fashionable in cooler seasons.

Plate II.236 (right) Detail from a fashion illustration of 1839 from 'The Ladies Cabinet' showing promenade dress. The voluminous shawl worn here has a triangular area of decoration in the bottom corner but the main field is plain, a common decorative scheme of the period. Not all shawls were of this size, nor were they all edged with gathered frills.

Plate II.237 (left) Triangular shawl: 1830s. This shawl is lined with pink silk taffeta: I have come across a number of different whiteworked accessories from about the 1820s-1840s lined with varying colours of silk taffeta but it is impossible to say how common the practice was at the time. The curving floral spray is similar to the discrete curved sprays of the mid 1820s-30s but rather more sprawling, as is the border. This and the contrast of bold flower heads with feathery leaves suggests a mid-late 1830s date.

Plate II.237a (right) *Detail of the border of the shawl in Plate II.237.*
The frill of hand-embroidered machine net is attached along straight edges each bordered by a buttonholed line and an openwork band between trailed lines.
The long, top edge, not shown, is finished with tiny points, an openwork line and a very narrow border pattern.
The only fillings are of ladder stitch and needlepoint.

Plate II.238 (right)
Triangular shawl: 1830s
This is a fairly small example with simple decoration but the embroidery is very similar in style to that of the shawl in Plate II.237, including the finishing of the long, top edge.
CB - 17½in (44.5cm);
L edge - 26½in (67.5cm);
D spray into corner - 9in (23cm);
D top border - ½in (1.5cm);
D main border - 1½in (4cm)
CB cut on the cross

Plate II.239 (left) *Triangular shawl: 1830s-40s*
The design has a distinctly oriental feel to it. This and the wide openwork borders suggest a late 1830s-40s date. The frill along the side edges is of whitework: the top edge is finished in the same way as the shawls in Plates II.237 and II.238.

Plate II.239a (below left) *Detail of the shawl in Plate II.239. This shawl is unfinished: the muslin bordering the buttonholed dentate edge of the frills has not been cut off. The embroidery is in padded satin stitch with outlined dots; whipped running and trailed lines; and pulled-thread fillings.*
Main panel CB - 33in (84cm); L edge - 40½in (103cm); D spray into corner - 17in (43cm); D top border - ⅝in (1.7cm); D main border - 4in including ¾in pulled-thread work (10cm inc. 2cm)
D frill - 3¾in (9.5cm); D pattern - 2in (5cm)
CB cut on the cross, frill on the straight

Plate II.240a (below right) *Detail of the shawl in Plate II.240.*

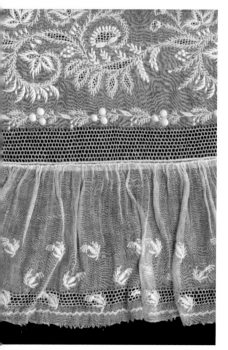

Plate II.240 *Triangular shawl: late 1830s-1840s. This is considerably larger than the other shawls shown and would look more like the shawl in Plate II.236 in wear. It is worked in a fine rococo design: the curvaceous orientalised leaves and scrolls forming the cartouches are in appliqué work, with flower heads and other smaller motifs in padded satin stitch. Pulled-thread work creates a border and fillings in imitation of Dresden work: this was worked before the second layer of fabric was applied. The edges are trimmed with a very narrow bobbin lace with picots. CB - 47in (119.5cm); L edge - 56in (142.5cm); D spray into corner - 17½in (44.5cm); Dmax top border - ¾in (2cm); Dmax main border - 3in (7.7cm); pulled band - ⅝in (1.5cm), CB cut on the cross. See Plates I.36, p25 and II.240a for details.*

Plate II.241 (left) Fashion illustration of August 1838. The midnight-blue mantle is wrapped tightly round the body with its long, shaped lappets hanging well down the front of the skirt. Although difficult to see, it has an extra frill or cape over the shoulders.

In addition to the shawls just seen, which comprise simple, flat panels of fabric with perhaps a gathered border, various shaped, seamed and gathered cloaks or mantles were worn in the later 1830s–1840s. Many had several layers, usually a long under layer that fell to waist level or below at the back with long, wide lappets at the front, and an additional shorter cape, pelerine or deep frill over the shoulders. The examples in the fashion illustrations in Plates II.241 and II.242, of 1838 and 1848, are typical of the enveloping quality of the mantle: that shown in Plate II.243 would look very similar when worn.

Plate II.243 (top right) This mantle has a deep pelerine or fichu seamed to the main body but has no other seams. Its frill is of needle-run machine net with a mesh imitating bobbin-made kat stitch. The design, with its dense padded satin stitch, contrasting feathery fronds and large areas of pulled fillings, dates this to about the second half of the 1830s. The edge is worked like the upper edges of triangular shawls shown previously: the frill is attached beneath the buttonholed points. Main body - CB - 21½ in (54cm (inc frill); half neck + front edge - 46in (117cm). Collar - CB - 11in (28cm); half neck - 22in (56cm). D frill - 3in (7.5cm); embroidered border 4.5in on body, 3.5in on collar, 1in down front (11.3cm; 8.7cm; 2.5cm).

Plate II.242 (top left) Fashion illustration of August 1848: Harris M & AG. Although the mantle shown here is larger than that in Plate II.241 either could have been worn from the late 1830s to late 1840s. The body of the mantle is coloured pink: this may suggest that it was intended to be made in white muslin lined with pink silk like the triangular shawl in Plate. II.237: the frill could be embroidered muslin or lace.

Plate II.243a (bottom left) Detail of the border and frill of the mantle in Plate II.243.

Plate II.243b (bottom right) Pattern for the mantle in Plate II.243.

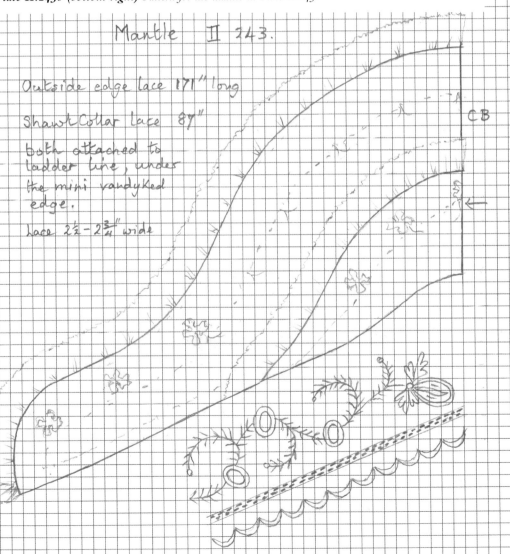

Mantle II 243.

Outside edge lace 171" long

Shawl Collar lace 87"

both attached to
ladder line, under
the mini vandyked
edge.

Lace 2½ - 2¾" wide

CB

Handkerchiefs

In previous pages there have been various references to 'handkerchiefs' and several have appeared in fashion illustrations from the 1820s onwards. The corners of two surviving examples have also been illustrated in Plates I.35 and II.182b. At 30in x 31½ in, the latter was of a size similar to that of many 18th century kerchiefs but appears to have been particularly large for its period. As will be seen from the following examples, decorative versions from the late 1830s - early 1840s seem to average about 20-24in square, though this is still much larger than the size of a modern woman's handkerchief.

The inclusion of these items in fashion illustrations, held elegantly in the hand, shows that they had an important display rôle: the finest are made from superb muslins or lawns and decorated with the most exquisite embroidery of their day. They were intended to demonstrate the wealth, position and taste of their owners. Unfortunately only a few examples can be shown here and these are of good - high quality: numerous handkerchiefs of similar size can be found in collections but many have far simpler decoration.

Plate II.244 (left) Corner of one of a group of three slightly different handkerchiefs all bearing the embroidered inscription 'E.B.Rudd 1838'. This is in a firm cotton fabric with a woven striped border. It is edged with a ¼in (0.6cm) - wide Buckinghamshire point bobbin lace.
23in x 24in (58.5cm x 61cm); E.B. Rudd - 5½in (14cm)

Plate II.245 a,b,c,d (opposite) Group of four corners from a single handkerchief. The very dense, bold style in which the motifs are worked suggests that this handkerchief dates from the 1830s.
It is worked in beautifully graduated padded satin stitch with embroidered net fillings. We have already seen that, in the 1830s, designers were trying to get away from the simple, repetitive designs that had been current for over 40 years and were looking for inspiration to all forms of old and foreign design styles, to treatises on science and art and, indeed, to any source of novelty which they could incorporate in their designs. 'Novelty' was the key and is seen in the four different arrangements in the corners of this handkerchief. A marriage is suggested by the two hearts with an arrow through them in one corner but what did the designer have in mind when he drew the motif at bottom right?
Handkerchief - 29in x 29½in (73.8cm x 75cm). Corner to parasol tip (Plate II.245c) 4in (10cm)

Plate II.246 *Page of patterns from the 'Journal des Demoiselles' of 1840*
The crowns, top left, are described as 'couronnes de fantaisie' for embroidery on a mother's handkerchief. Bottom centre is a design for a cuff: the oriental pavilion at bottom right is for a handkerchief corner: the four corner designs are for a handkerchief sachet.

Plate II.247 (right) *Handkerchief corner with a basket of roses above a rococo leaf design, both similar to designs in Plate II.246. The corner design occupies a 3¾in square (9.5cm).*

Plates II.248 (below left), II.248a (below right) *Two corners from a handkerchief: the other two corners (not shown) have different designs in a similar floral style; 1830s-40s.*
The edge is rolled outside a line of drawn-thread work and trimmed with a very fine Valenciennes bobbin lace. The work is in various forms of padded satin stitch with trailed lines, overcast eyelets and pulled fillings.
Handkerchief size - 24in x 23½ in (61cm x 59.7cm)
Corner motifs occupy 3¾in squares (9.5cm x 9.5cm)
D lace - 1in (2.5cm)

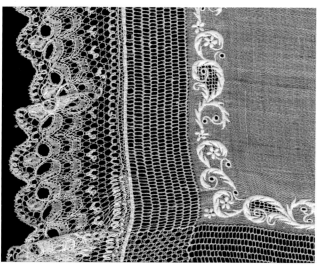

Plate II.249 (above) *Detail from a page of patterns from the 'Journal des Demoiselles' of 1841.*
Associated text states that the collar and two corner designs are for whitework embroidery: the handkerchief designs are to be continued round the entire periphery and to be bordered by drawn work and a lace trimming: the spot designs are for morning bonnets.

Plate II.250 (left) *Detail from a handkerchief: probably early 1840s. This handkerchief has a design right round the edge which is very similar to the right-hand pattern in Plate II.249 and also accords with the instructions in being bordered by a broad band of drawn work and a bobbin lace trimming: there is no other decoration. 27½in square (70cm x 70cm); D drawn work - ⅞in (2.2cm); D embroidery - ¾in (2cm)*
D lace - 1⅝in (4.2cm) (kat stitch ground; probably English East Midlands)

Plate II.251 (right) *Detail from a handkerchief: late 1830s-40s: Museum of Somerset, Taunton, Cat. No. OSDD 3098 This oriental horseman is superbly worked in a variety of stitches to create texture and detail. This design occupies 2 corners: the other two are occupied by a tiger attacking a snake. The handkerchief (21in x 20½in (54.5cm x 52cm) has a 1in-wide (2.5cm) drawn border and ¾in - wide (2cm) Valenciennes bobbin lace trimming (not shown).*

Plate II.252 (bottom right) *Handkerchief corner: late 1830s-40s. All four corners of this handkerchief have the same design which continues as a very narrow border along the sides. 22in x 22¾in (56cm x 58cm); D lace 1½in (4cm); D - drawn work - ¼in (0.6cm): length shown excluding lace - 6½in (16.5cm)*

Plate II.252a (below) *Detail of the handkerchief corner in Plate II.252.*

Plate II.253 (above) *Handkerchief corner: late 1830s-40s*
*The superbly-worked embroidery design continues along all four
sides of this handkerchief. The coiling stems and tendrils of the
trailing vine bear a strong resemblance to those in the collar design
of 1839 in Plate II.145.*
*The lace is a point ground bobbin lace of a type which has come to be
called 'Regency' lace but is of a design that was not in fact made until
about the 1830s: it may be of English or continental manufacture.*
21in x 20¾in (53.3cm x 52.7cm)
D lace 2in (5cm); D whitework - 1½in (4cm)

Plate II.253a (left) *Detail of the handkerchief in Plate II.253.*
*Much of the work is in heavily padded trailing with counted thread
(not pulled or drawn) fillings: these are meticulously worked and show
merely as slight differences in texture to the naked eye. The eyelets
have needlepoint wheel fillings. This may be continental work.*

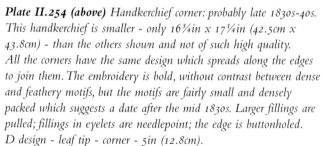

Plate II.254 (above) *Handkerchief corner: probably late 1830s-40s. This handkerchief is smaller - only 16¾in x 17¼in (42.5cm x 43.8cm) - than the others shown and not of such high quality. All the corners have the same design which spreads along the edges to join them. The embroidery is bold, without contrast between dense and feathery motifs, but the motifs are fairly small and densely packed which suggests a date after the mid 1830s. Larger fillings are pulled; fillings in eyelets are needlepoint; the edge is buttonholed. D design - leaf tip - corner - 5in (12.8cm).*

Plate II.255 (top right) *Handkerchief corner: late 1830s-40s This corner is decorated with fine Ayrshire work with needlepoint fillings: the other corners are plain. Sadly the handkerchief is in poor condition and has lost its lace border. 22½in x 23¼in (57cm x 59cm): L shown - 8in (20.5cm)*

Plate II.255a (right) *Detail of the handkerchief in Plate II.255.*

Plate II. 256 (right) *Handkerchief corner: probably 1840s*
All corners are the same. The very fine embroidery is more complex
than in most other examples: dense areas are in satin stitch, padded
satin stitch and shadow stitch with dots worked over the surface.
Fillings are pulled: lines are in heavily padded trailing with very
fine lines in whipped running. The use of satin stitch and shadow
stitch makes the work look flatter than most other whiteworks of the
period. This is high-quality professional work and may be
continental. 21½in (54.5cm) square; L design from muslin corner
along edge – 6¾in (17.2cm).

Plate II.256a *Detail of the handkerchief corner in Plate II.256. The edges are rolled outside a drawn-thread line and trimmed with*
Valenciennes bobbin lace.

Plate II.257 (right) *Handkerchief: probably 1840s*
This is unusual in having corner motifs in two different designs and a separate motif (the same design) in the centre of each side.
The edge is buttonholed outside a band of drawn work and trimmed with Buckinghamshire point bobbin lace.
The work is similar to that of the handkerchief in Plate II.256 but not as fine: dense areas are mainly in shadow stitch with backstitched dots worked over the surface.
22in x 22in (56cm x 56cm); D drawn band - ½in (1.3cm); D lace - 1½in (4cm)

Plate II.257a (bottom right) *Detail from the handkerchief in Plate II.257.*

Plate II.258 (below) *Detail from a handkerchief corner. This is from the same handkerchief as the lion in Plate I.35.*

GLOSSARY PART II: General decoration, costume, fabric and sewing terms other than embroidery terms

Ayrshire work See Glossary of Embroidery terms

Baroque A bold design style originating in the 17th century with a strong sense of movement characterised, in embroidery and lace, by large flowers, leaves and fruits, often of an exotic nature, carried on undulating or scrolling stems and sometimes interwoven with decorated ribbons or strapwork.

Blonde lace A bobbin lace worked in natural cream-coloured silk thread.

Bobbin lace Any hand-made lace made with a multitude of threads each carried on a bobbin; the bobbins are manipulated to cross and twist the threads together to create the lace fabric.

Brussels lace A bobbin or needlepoint lace worked in small pieces joined in a variety of ways, sometimes with the two techniques mixed.

Buffon/buffont A voluminous handkerchief worn puffed up under the chin.

Calico/calicot Originally a cotton fabric from Calcutta, India but used generally for fine cottons or some cotton/linen mixes of a closer weave than muslin.

Cambric Originally a fine linen fabric from Cambrai in Flanders but used generally for fine linens or even, in the 19th century, for cottons.

Canezou A waist-length, sleeveless jacket but the usage of the term and shape of article were quite varied.

Cartouche A decorative frame formed by various curved shapes.

Chemisette (Also known as a habit shirt or blouse at different periods) A woman's accessory or garment made to cover the upper part of the body, filling or partly filling a low neckline of a dress, usually sleeveless and not seamed beneath the arms: originally termed a habit shirt from its use under a riding habit and derivation from a man's shirt.

Cut on the cross Cut across the grain of a fabric, i.e. diagonal to the warp of a woven fabric.

Cut on the straight Cut in line with the grain of a fabric, i.e. parallel to the warp or, less commonly, the weft of a woven fabric.

Dorset button Any of several types of button made particularly in Dorset, including fabric-covered metal rings, rings covered with threads wound diametrally in a wheel pattern, conical padded buttons, etc.

Draw-string A tape or cord housed in a fabric casing but with its ends free. The fabric can be 'drawn up', or gathered, on the draw-string.

Dresden lace/work See Glossary of Embroidery terms

Fichu A common 19th century term for a roughly triangular accessory worn around the shoulders with long ends hanging down the front but the usage of the term and shape of article were quite varied.

Fichu-pelerine Originally a pelerine with long ends hanging down the front: later known simply as a pelerine.

Gauged/ing Gathered by at least two sets of running stitches into very small, even pleats.

Gigot French term for 'leg o' mutton' used to describe sleeves which are very full on the shoulder and upper arm but tight on the lower arm.

Habit shirt See 'Chemisette'.

Half-handkerchief A triangular piece of fabric formed by cutting a square in half diagonally: worn round the neck or over the head.

Handkerchief A square of fabric often folded in half diagonally and worn like a half-handkerchief or a slightly smaller square carried in the hand but these were generally specified as 'pocket handkerchiefs'.

Insertion A narrow strip of lace or other decorative fabric usually with two straight edges intended to be sewn between two panels of fabric as a decorative join.

Kerchief Alternative name for a handkerchief or neckerchief worn round the neck.

Lawn Originally a fine, plain-weave linen fabric, and used here with that meaning, but often used for fine cotton fabrics.

Lappet A hanging piece or streamer: a term usually associated with the streamers hanging from the back or sides of a cap but also applicable to long ends of fichus, pelerines and similar accessories.

Leg o' mutton See **'Gigot'**.

Modesty piece A small panel of fabric used to fill in a low neckline or a frill of fine fabric standing up from the neckline, partly filling the décolletage.

Muslin Fine, plain-weave cotton varying from a very soft, open-weave fabric to a slightly firmer fabric.

Needlepoint/needlepoint lace Any lace made by hand solely with a needle and thread. The basic stitch is usually a buttonhole stitch but the stitch and the way stitches interlink can be varied to give different effects.

Neo-classical A style inspired by ancient Greek, Roman and Etruscan artefacts characterised, in women's dress, by a high waist, slim line and flowing drapery and, in decoration, by bands of repeated, symmetrical motifs or simple, repetitive, linear decoration. Certain motifs, such as the anthemium (honeysuckle), laurel, Greek key and spiral designs, are particularly common.

Pelerine Originally a large, wide collar which spreads across the shoulders but the usage of the term and shape of article were quite varied. See also **'Fichu-pelerine'**.

Pina cloth A fine, crisp, semi-transparent fabric woven from pina fibres from the leaves of members of the pineapple plant family.

Pocket handkerchief See **'Handkerchief'**.

Point ground A fine bobbin-made net with six-sided meshes used in Buckinghamshire point and some continental bobbin laces.

Pounce A powder used for dusting through holes along lines in a pattern to transfer the design to an underlying fabric or other medium.

Rococo A design style derived in the 18th century from the baroque but lighter and more playful in character, with much asymmetry, fantasy and decorative detail in its motifs, characterised, in embroidery and lace, by leafy, floral designs with scrolling and branching stems and tendrils

Selvedge The firm longitudinal edge of a woven fabric.

Shawl The late-18th - early-19th century term for a rectangle of fabric of much greater length than width, now more usually called a stole; also used in the 19th century for a large square or triangle of fabric worn round the shoulders.

Spot A term used not just for round dots but also for tiny leaf or flower motifs used in regular arrays to decorate plain fabrics.

Strapwork Decorative bands or ribbons in a design.

Tambour frame (from the French 'tambour' for drum) A circular frame for stretching fabric for embroidering; particularly used for chain stitch worked with a hooked tambour needle.

Tambour hook Name used for a hooked needle for 'tambouring' i.e. creating chain stitches on a fabric: it has a pointed tip for piercing the fabric.

Turnover design A design, usually on a fabric square, which is worked on opposite sides of the fabric on the two triangular halves so that, when the fabric is folded on the diagonal for wear, the right side of the work is uppermost on both halves.

Valenciennes bobbin lace A very fine bobbin lace worked in long lengths: unlike Buckinghamshire point lace, it has no thick threads outlining the motifs.

Vandyked/ing A term used to describe a pointed or scalloped edging after the artist Anthony van Dyck whose early 17th century portraits show many lace edgings of this character. Many vandyked edges comprise tiny points or scallops (less than 0.5in or 1cm wide) worked on larger points or scallops.

Vermicular 'Worm-like' or meandering.

SELECT BIBLIOGRAPHY

A Lady, *The Workwoman's Guide,* 1840, Bloomfield Books reprint, 1975

Arnold, J, *Patterns of Fashion I,* Macmillan, 1972

Ashelford, J, *The Art of Dress: Clothes and Society 1500-1914,* National Trust Enterprises Ltd., 1996

Baker, J, M, *The Moravians: an alternative perspective on whitework embroidery 1780-1850,* M.A. Thesis held in the Winchester School of Art (Southampton University) Library

Boyle, E, *The Irish Flowerers,* Ulster Folk Museum 1971

Bradfield, N, *Costume in Detail, Women's dress 1730-1930,* Harrap, 1981

Bryson, A, F, *Ayrshire Needlework,* Batsford, 1989

Burton, A, *The Rise and Fall of King Cotton,* British Broadcasting Corpn, 1984

Byrde, P, *Jane Austen Fashion: Fashion and Needlework in the works of Jane Austen,* Excellent Press, 1999

Byrde, P, *Nineteenth Century Fashion,* Batsford, 1992

Clabburn, P, *The Needleworker's Dictionary,* Macmillan, 1976

Cunnington, C, W, *English Women's Clothing in the 19th Century,* Faber, & Faber, 1937

Davidson, C, *The World of Mary Ellen Best,* Chatto & Windus, 1985

Davis, D, *A History of Shopping,* Routledge & K. Paul, 1966

de Dillmont, T, *Encyclopedia of Needlework,* D.M.C., Mulhouse

Earnshaw, P, *Lace Machines and Machine Laces,* Batsford, 1986

Foster, V, *A Visual History of Costume: The Nineteenth Century,* Batsford

Four Hundred Years of Fashion, V&A /Collins, 1984

Gibbs-Smith, *The Fashionable Lady in the 19th Century,* V&A, 1960

Godfrey, F, P, *An International History of the Sewing Machine,* Robert Hale, 1982

Gostelow, M, *A World of Embroidery,* Mills & Boon, 1975

Harris, B (Ed), *Famine and Fashion: Needlewomen in the Nineteenth Century,* Ashgate, 2005

Head, C, *Old Sewing Machines,* Shire Album 84

Holland, V, *Hand Coloured Fashion Plates 1770-1899,* Batsford, 1955

Iklé, E, *La Broderie Mécanique, 1828-1930,* Editions A. Calavais

Lansbury, L, *Whitework,* The Royal School of Needlework, 2012

Levey, S, M, *Lace: a History,* V&A/Maney, 1983

Mackrell, A, *Shawls, Stoles and Scarves, (Costume Accessories Series),* Batsford, 1986

Marsh, G, *18th Century Embroidery Techniques,* Guild of Master Craftsmen Publications Ltd., 2006

Marsh, G, *19th Century Embroidery Techniques,* Guild of Master Craftsmen Publications Ltd., 2008

Moore, D L, *Fashion through Fashion Plates, 1770-1970,* Ward Lock, 1971

Morris, B, *Victorian Embroidery,* Herbert Jenkins, 1962

Paine, S, *Chikan Embroidery: the floral whitework of India,* Shire

Ribeiro, A, *The Gallery of Fashion,* National Portrait Gallery, 2000

Swain, M, *The Flowerers: the Story of Ayrshire Needlework,* W&R Chambers, 1955

Swain, M, *Scottish Embroidery, Medieval to Modern,* Batsford, 1986

Swain, M, *Ayrshire and other Whitework,* Shire, 1982

Swain, M, *Historical Needlework: a study of Influences in Scotland and Northern England,* Barrie & Jenkins, 1970

Tarrant, N, *The Rise and Fall of the Sleeve, 1825-40,* Royal Scottish Museum, Edinburgh

Toomer, H, *Antique Lace: Identifying Types and Techniques,* Schiffer, 2001

Toomer, H, *Baby wore white: Robes for special occasions 1800-1910,* Heather Toomer Antique Lace, 2004

Toomer, H, *Embroidered with white: the 18th century fashion for Dresden lace and other whiteworked accessories,* Heather Toomer Antique Lace, 2008

Wardle, P, *Guide to English Embroidery,* V&A, 1970

Waugh, N, *The Cut of Women's Clothes, 1600-1930,* Faber & Faber, 1968

PUBLIC COLLECTIONS CONTAINING WHITEWORKED ACCESSORIES AND RELATED MATERIAL

Most good costume collections in UK museums contain some whiteworked accessories but there are rarely many on display and they are often too far away or too dimly lit for fine detail to be visible: the same applies to Continental costume and textile collections.

It is worth contacting such museums in advance of a visit to arrange to see material in store. It is also worth asking at your local museum and, when travelling, to keep an eye open for special exhibitions or small, local museums, particularly in textile areas, as these often have specialist collections. I have often stumbled across little publicised but fascinating examples in this way.

Costume collections often also contain original fashion magazines, plates and/or other documentary material while reference libraries, both local authority and university, are a further source of such material. The staff of all such institutions have invariably been helpful in suggesting material for study, retrieving it from store and facilitating research.

The list of institutions with costume collections or other archival material given under 'Acknowledgments' indicates many of the UK's better collections but is by no means exhaustive. Cities in important textile areas, such as Bedford, Leeds, Halifax, Leicester, Nottingham, and Norwich, and major cities, such as Birmingham, Belfast, Edinburgh and Newcastle, to name just a few, all have costume or textile collections that are worth investigating.

The Royal School of Needlework and Embroiderers Guild also have their own collections and provide courses on whitework embroidery.

ACCESSORY AND EMBROIDERY PATTERNS TO BE FOUND IN THIS WORK

Original 19th-century embroidery patterns - pp30, 31, 32, 33, 39, 50, 51, 61, 64, 77, 78, 113, 114, 130, 136, 138, 143, 149, 159, 178, 180

Scale patterns for accessories:
Apron - p56
Canezou - pp73, 83, 89, 157
Cape - p162
Chemisette/habit shirt - pp44, 75, 125, 127, 141
Collar/small pelerine - pp73, 75, 119
Cuff - p100
Fichu - pp108
Larger pelerine - pp83, 101, 108
Mantle - p175

INDEX

In the index, references are indicated as follows: text - page nos. in standard type: captions - page nos. in italics; plates - plate nos. in italics